A SUFFICIENT
Grace

Other J. Oswald Sanders books available from
Discovery House Publishers:

Dynamic Spiritual Leadership
Enjoying Intimacy with God
Enjoying Your Best Years
Every Life Is a Plan of God
Facing Loneliness
Heaven: Better by Far
Prayer Power Unlimited

Discovery House Publishers

Books, music, and videos that feed the soul with the Word of God

Box 3566 Grand Rapids, MI 49501

A SUFFICIENT Grace

BREAKTHROUGH TO SPIRITUAL
AND EMOTIONAL HEALTH

J. OSWALD SANDERS

A Sufficient Grace:
Breakthrough to Spiritual and Emotional Health
© 2003 by the estate of J. Oswald Sanders.
All rights reserved.

Original edition published as *Spiritual Therapy* ©1991.

Discovery House Publishers is affiliated with
RBC Ministries, Grand Rapids, Michigan 49501.

Discovery House books are distributed to the trade exclusively
by Barbour Publishing, Inc., Uhrichsville, OH 44683.

Unless otherwise indicated, Scripture is taken from
the *Holy Bible, New International Version* (NIV).

Interior design by Sherri L. Hoffman

Library of Congress Cataloging-in-Publication Data

Sanders, J. Oswald (John Oswald), 1902-
    A Sufficient Grace: finding emotional health amid stress and suffer-
ing / by J. Oswald Sanders.
       p.   cm.
    ISBN: 0-57293-121-3
    Christian life. I. Title.
BV4501.3.S255 2003
248.4—dc22   2003020710

04 05 06 07 08 09 // DP // 10 9 8 7 6 5 4 3 2
Printed in the United States of America

Contents

Publisher's Foreword

*W*e are pleased to be able to publish this new edition of a work by J. Oswald Sanders that was originally published as *A Spiritual Clinic,* then later revised by the author and published as *Spiritual Therapy*. In his preface to *Spiritual Therapy,* the author wrote the following:

> A continuing inquiry for *A Spiritual Clinic* since it went out of print some years ago has encouraged me to rewrite it completely and re-issue it under a title that more exactly conveys the thrust of the book: *Spiritual Therapy.*
>
> In the rewriting I have been impressed with the fact that it deals with matters that are even more characteristic of these days than of those when it was first written—depression, tension, stress, suffering, justice, spiritual warfare, money, ambition, life's handicaps.
>
> In each case I have endeavored to relate the problem to both Scripture and the contemporary scene. The thesis of the book is that the stresses and problems faced by Christian workers in this confused age will find their answer not in tranquilizers and stimulants, but in a correct understanding and application of the relevant scriptural principles. Success and effectiveness in ministry are the natural outcome of conformity to spiritual laws enunciated in the Scriptures.

In the final analysis, however, there is but one basic solution to life's complex problems—correct relation with and obedience to the Triune God, who is adequate for every emergency and competent to deal with the intricacies of every yearning and troubled heart.

J. Oswald Sanders
Auckland, New Zealand
1991

CHAPTER 1

How God Deals with Depression

"Put me to death right now" (NUMBERS 11:15).

"I have had enough, LORD. . . . Take my life"
(1 KINGS 19:4).

"Take away my life, for it is better for me to die
than to live" (JONAH 4:3).

The psalms of David, it has been said, contain the whole music of the heart of man, swept by the hand of his Maker. "In them are gathered the lyrical outburst of his tenderness, the moan of his penitence, the pathos of his sorrow" (source unknown).

When he posed the question to himself, "Why are you downcast, O my soul? Why so disturbed within me?" (Psalm 42:11), the psalmist was only giving expression to a malady of the soul which few Christians are spared. Even the mighty Paul, with all his experience of God's love and grace, was not exempt from the experience. "God, who comforts the downcast," he testified, "comforted [me] by the coming of Titus" (2 Corinthians 7:6).

We are not promised automatic immunity from the experience of depression or despondency simply because we are believers. If we violate natural or spiritual laws, God usually allows them to take their course. We need only to read Bible biographies to find confirmation of this.

In addition, we have a very astute and vastly experienced adversary whose threefold objective is, in the apt words of Ruth Paxson, to despoil us of our wealth, to decoy us from our walk with God, and to disable us for warfare. To achieve this end, he has no more potent weapon in his arsenal than depression or despondency.

Who of us has not at times experienced that nebulous, indefinable yet painfully real feeling of misery and hopelessness? There is some consolation in the knowledge that we are not alone in our pain. Other godly men and women have trodden the same shadowed pathway before us, have felt as we do, and yet have emerged into the sunshine of God's comforting and strengthening love once more. Let us consider some examples from the Bible.

Three Unanswered Prayers

Is it not revealing that three of God's most successful prophets fell prey to depression and despondency? Perhaps it was their very prominence and success that caused God to select them as audiovisuals for us lesser mortals. In each case, their despondency went so deep that they wanted to die. Only a desperately serious case of depression would rob a prophet of his desire to live. The first who asked God that he might die was

Moses the Meek

This brilliant and richly gifted man had achieved great things for God and his nation. For long he had endured the incessant complaining of the Israelites and carried unbelievably heavy burdens. Under his charismatic leadership, a rabble of slaves had become an organized nation. Time and again they had experienced God's miraculous intervention and provision; but their persistent discontent so depressed Moses that he cried to God in his anguish:

> "They keep wailing to me, 'Give us meat to eat!' I cannot carry all these people by myself; the burden is too heavy for me. If this is how you are going to treat me, *put me to death right now* . . . and do not let me face my own ruin" (NUMBERS 11:13–15, emphasis added).

Overburdened as he was with the fickleness of his fellow-countrymen, Moses was overwhelmed with a sense of complete and utter failure. He overlooked the fact that God has made us responsible only for our own maturity, not for that of others. In his despair, he little dreamed that God had years of fruitful service ahead for him.

Elijah the Dramatic

Everything Elijah did seemed to be in Technicolor. He was fresh from the drama and victory of Mount Carmel. In it he had figured as the divine instrument in turning the nation back from idolatry to God. The heathen god, Baal, had been thoroughly discredited and its priests destroyed. (1 Kings 18:19–40).

Then suddenly Elijah wilted. His amazing courage failed and he fled for his life from the wrath of the queen he had so recently courageously defied. Under the lonely broom tree he mourned:

> ". . . and *prayed that he might die.* 'I have had enough, LORD,' he said. 'Take my life; I am no better than my ancestors'" (1 KINGS 19:4, emphasis added).

Jonah the Disobedient

After his rebellious flight from the call of duty, and his subsequent sub-marine experience, Jonah repented and obeyed God. In response to his faithful proclamation of the impending divine judgment on wicked and cruel Nineveh, to the prophet's amazement and dismay he saw the whole city turn to God, repenting in sackcloth and ashes. True to His nature, when He saw their repentance, God had compassion upon them, "and did not bring upon them the destruction he had threatened" (Jonah 3:10).

Instead of leaping with joy at this display of divine mercy, Jonah was dismayed at the success of his mission. Under the gourd that had sprung up he moaned:

> "I knew that you are a gracious and compassionate God, slow to anger and abounding in love, a God who relents from sending calamity. Now, O LORD, *take away my life,* for it is better for me to die than to live" (JONAH 4:2–3, emphasis added).

Strange logic, this! But when we are depressed and despondent, cold logic is not our forte.

Diagnosis of Depression and Despondency

An analysis of the circumstances that gave rise to these three unanswered prayers is revealing. Is it not surprising that in each case the prophet had more cause for elation than depression?

Had Moses not seen God's mighty power operate through his instrumentality in Egypt and in the desert? Had Elijah not witnessed the visible manifestation of God's presence and power on Mount Carmel? Had Jonah not been the reluctant instrument in the greatest mass turning to God in recorded history? Then why this despair and despondency?

We never know when our tireless enemy will launch this devastating guided missile against us. It may come when there seems least reason for it, as in these cases. But, usually, preexisting conditions allow him to get a foothold.

It seems as though a similar threefold background contributed to the misery of each of these men:

A Physiological Reason

The unremitting strain of administration and adjudication for the whole nation had greatly overtaxed *Moses'* reserves of physical and nervous energy. To maintain liaison between a large nation of discontented people and God was a superhuman task. But on his own confession, he had been trying to carry it alone (Numbers 11:13–15).

When his father-in-law, Jethro, saw the toll that this work was taking on Moses in his valiant attempts to fulfill his ministry, Jethro gave him sound advice—that he share the task with suitably qualified men. He should retain the leadership and legislative role, and delegate lower judicial functions to these chosen men. Moses acted on Jethro's advice, and catastrophe was averted.

The lesson for overburdened leaders—and other people too—is that we ourselves are not always the best judges of the cost at which we exercise our ministry. (The author writes from painful experience.) Often we do not realize when our reserves of physical and nervous energy are seriously overdrawn. Although we may not appreciate the advice of our Jethros, they may be God's messengers to us, and we are wise to weigh their counsel carefully.

Then consider the emotional strain and stress involved in *Elijah's* lone encounter with the priests of Baal on Mount Carmel. Add to that the intensity of his praying, the twenty-mile

run to Jezreel, the subsequent flight from Jezebel, and his
abstinence from food (1 Kings 18:40–46). The man was totally exhausted emotionally and physically, and quite unfit to meet
the threats of the raging Jezebel.

Jonah's depression, too, had a physical basis. C. C. Dobson
suggests that part of his trouble was a touch of sunstroke. Emotionally spent and physically exhausted after his unpopular witness to a city of 1.5 million people, and affected by the heat of
the eastern sun, the despondent prophet limped out of the city
and erected a shelter from its burning rays. But after the with-
ering of the gourd that God had prepared to shelter him, "the
sun blazed on Jonah's head so that he grew faint" (Jonah 4:8).

Such were the physical causes of the collapse of the three
great prophets. But there was a second reason for their depression and despondency.

A Self-Centered Reason

Until the moment of his collapse, *Moses* had been singularly selfless in his care for his people. Indeed, when God's anger
was kindled against the idolatrous nation, Moses had asked
Him to blot out his own name from God's book if only the people might be spared (Exodus 32:32). But now he descended to
a lower level. Forgetful of the desperate spiritual need of the
nation, he even reproached God, and indulged in an orgy of self-
pity. He lost sight of all God had done for and through him, and
became self-engrossed.

Elijah too, in his time of reaction reproached God in strange
self-disillusionment and said, "I am no better than my ances-
tors." His self-esteem had been dealt a shattering blow. "I have
been very zealous for the LORD God Almighty," he complained,
implying that in spite of all his zeal, God had let him down.

Twice he repeated the plaintive, "I am the only one left" (1 Kings 19:10, 14). He was engulfed in self-pity.

Nor was the case different with *Jonah.* His reason for reproaching God was resentment of His mercy and forbearance with Nineveh. But the real trouble was that when God spared Nineveh the judgment Jonah had announced, He had dealt the prophet's reputation a shattering blow. Jonah had prophesied judgment, but God had exercised mercy. Since Jonah's reputation was now in tatters, it would be better to die than to live. But there was also

A Spiritual Reason

These were true men of God, so there was another dimension to their lives. Neither the physical nor the selfish elements was the sole cause of their depression. In each case there was a deep spiritual disappointment, and a sense of personal failure.

Beneath *Moses'* outburst lay a sense of being out of touch with God (Numbers 11:11–15)—a common feeling when one is depressed. Coupled with this was keen disappointment at the renewed murmuring and discontent of the Israelites. He was a failure! Too small for the task! Better to die than witness the failure of the whole project!

Elijah had longed and prayed for a sweeping and permanent revival of true religion in his loved nation, but to his dismay the fair promise of Carmel seemed to vanish once the long-denied rain had fallen. The stirring had been only evanescent and superficial. Mistakenly, he thought he was alone in his zeal for God. He was an abject failure, and death was preferable to life under such conditions.

Jonah's repentance and subsequent prophetic ministry to mighty Nineveh had been a courageous and costly effort. He had obeyed the Lord and delivered the message that in forty days Nineveh would be overthrown because of its wickedness and cruelty. And then, because there had been national repentance, God had relented and thus had let him down. How could he ever face people again—a discredited prophet?

The worst of it was that in his heart of hearts Jonah had known that this would happen. Had he himself not experienced God's forgiving grace? How could he be sure the same would not happen again? How could he be sure of his message? He was a failure as a prophet and might as well end it all.

Prescription for Depression and Despondency

God's method of treatment for each of His overwrought servants is an unveiling of His personal and tender compassion. In not one case did He rebuke or chide them, nor did He answer their prayers. He knew their true motivation and perceived that their petitions were merely an understandable, though deluded, expression of self-pity. For each He had the appropriate remedy.

For *Moses* God prescribed the help of seventy capable and Spirit-filled elders, who would share his burden, thus freeing him for the higher responsibilities of leadership (Exodus 18:17–24). He gave Moses a fresh commission and renewed His promise: "Is the LORD's arm too short? You will now see whether or not what I say will come true for you" (Numbers 11:23).

The treatment for *Elijah* was, first, withdrawal to a solitary place where God could speak to him alone and reveal Himself afresh. Then two long sleeps, two meals of bread baked in God's kitchen, and long draughts of water drawn from the wells of heaven. Then God offered the encouraging assurance that, far from being alone, Elijah had the moral support of seven thousand others who had never bowed the knee to Baal, and of these one was given him for a companion (1 Kings 19:5–8).

For *Jonah* the Lord prepared a fast-growing gourd for shelter. Through Jonah's petulant pity for the gourd when it withered (Jonah 4:6–9), and his callous unconcern for the now repentant Nineveh, God revealed His divine solicitude and pity for those who turned from their wicked ways.

Contemporary Lessons

These Old Testament biographies enshrine principles that are equally relevant in the space age. In this connection Paul wrote: "These things happened to them as examples and were written down as warnings for us, on whom the fulfillment of the ages has come" (1 Corinthians 10:11). The episodes we have been studying are replete with lessons that are singularly appropriate in this pressured age. Here are some:

- Even honored servants of God cannot break His physical laws with impunity, nor are they immune from the onslaughts of depression and despondency.
- Over-expenditure of physical and nervous capital, even in desperately needy areas in God's service, gives our satanic adversary opportunity to attack our spirits. We recklessly overspend at our peril.
- Despondency can follow success as well as failure.
- If we are not to be put to flight by the adversary, we must allow time in our routine for physical and spiritual renewal.
- If we shift our center from God to self for even a short time, we lay ourselves open to this malady of the spirit.

- Delegation of some tasks, and dropping some commitments of secondary importance, will often bring a resurgence of optimism. We should give weight to the advice of our Jethros.
- Physical precautions can prevent sunstroke, malaria, and other afflictions.
- Going to bed earlier and getting more rest, coupled with a balanced diet, will settle many a case of depression. "I have so much to do," said the French philosopher, Le Maistre, "that I must go to bed."
- God prescribes individually for each of His patients.
- Discouragement over the apparent failure of our best efforts, if not met with the shield of faith (Ephesians 6:16), can react disastrously on our spirits and degenerate into self-pity and despair. Such failure is often more apparent than real, as was the case with Elijah.
- God delights to restore His depressed or despondent children and give them a sphere of increased usefulness.

CHAPTER 2

Is There a Purpose in Suffering?

"There was given me a thorn in my flesh. . . ."

*"My grace is sufficient for you, for my power
is made perfect in weakness"
(2 CORINTHIANS 12:7, 9).*

Some questions are so perplexing that we may need the
humility to be willing to live with them unanswered fully,
and not demand complete intellectual satisfaction. One such is
the enigma of suffering. Why is there so much suffering in the
world? And in particular, why do the righteous suffer?

This subject has exercised the minds of men and women of
all eras. The findings of some have shed facets of light, but after
ages of inquiry and discussion, no one has come up with a
wholly satisfying answer. The book that has shed the greatest
light on it is the Bible. In this connection Margaret Clarkson, in
her book *Destined for Glory,* has this to say:

> The Word of God *does* have answers to the problem
> of human pain, difficult as that problem is. They will
> not be found without much searching, but if we are
> willing to seek them diligently, we shall find them. We
> may not discover all the answers we should like, but we
> shall find all we really need to know.

A study of Paul's "third heaven" experience will throw some light on *the purpose of suffering*. In 2 Corinthians 12:1–10 we are granted an intimate glimpse into his inner life, and for this privilege we are indebted to those critics whose repeated challenge to his apostleship compelled him to bare his heart. Only the necessity of vindicating his office induced him to share such intimacies with his loved Corinthians.

In his defense, Paul tells of two conflicting experiences; one with its temptation to *elation*, the other with its tendency to *depression*. Then he shows how these contrasting experiences were brought into equilibrium by a single sentence from the Lord of glory.

The Paradise Experience

"I know a man in Christ who. . . . was caught up to paradise. He heard inexpressible things, things that man is not permitted to tell" (2 CORINTHIANS 12:2, 4).

Paradise is a Persian word meaning a walled garden. When a Persian king would honor someone, he would make him a "Companion of the Garden." That person was then privileged to walk in the royal gardens in company with the king. This was Paul's experience.

Some experiences are so rare and unique that they cannot be compassed in human language. But such an ecstatic experience carried its own dangers, and exposed even Paul to the peril of succumbing to spiritual pride. He was conscious of this when he wrote: "To keep me from becoming conceited . . . there was given me a thorn in my flesh" (2 Corinthians 12:7). God has His own way of training His messengers. In this case He erected a fence at the top of the precipice rather than providing an ambulance at the bottom.

Nothing so tends to inflate a person with a sense of his or her own importance as the possession of great gifts of intellect or the enjoyment of special and unusual experiences. And nothing more surely disqualifies someone for spiritual usefulness than pride. The very abundance of Paul's revelations could easily have isolated him from the very people to whom he was sent to minister. So God brought an equalizing factor into his life, lest his ministry become limited.

A real danger lies in recounting our own deeper spiritual experiences, especially our successes. Aware of this, an evangelist friend of mine declined to tell the remarkable story of his life. He realized the subtle temptation to filch some of the glory that belonged to God alone. So jealous was he that the power of the Spirit might continue to rest on his ministry, that he made a practice of trying to forget his past successes.

Peter, James, and John, our Lord's three intimates, were not permitted to encamp on the Mount of Transfiguration. They had to exchange the vision glorious for the convulsions of a demon-possessed boy. So Paul had to descend into the valley if he was to become God's messenger to distraught humanity. He had to learn that the mountain is only as high as the valley is deep. The higher he ascended in spiritual experience, the more deeply he had to be identified with his crucified Lord.

A Thorn in the Flesh

The Greek word for *thorn* can mean either a stake that pegs one to the ground, or a splinter, a thorn that constantly irritates. It conveys the idea of something sharp and painful that strikes deeply into the flesh. It would seem that the effect of its presence was to "cripple Paul's enjoyment of life, and to frustrate his full efficiency by draining his energies."

Paul is intentionally vague about this autobiographical glimpse. He is silent about the character or location of paradise, about the words he heard, and the visions he saw. He is especially uncommunicative as to the nature of this "thorn."

We should be grateful that he turns our attention away from the incidental and concentrates on unchanging principles of universal application. Had he specified his personal thorn, and it differed from ours, we would be less ready to believe that the divine compensation he enjoyed might be ours also. In the plan of God, Paul's was to be a representative case from which believers in all ages could draw comfort and strength.

Attempts to identify the thorn have been legion, all of them equally inconclusive. Some people have suggested these: spiritual temptations, doubt, depression, blasphemous suggestions, sensual temptations, persecution. But these do not seem to fit the case. Since it was a thorn "in the flesh," a continuing physical malady such as malaria, ophthalmia, or migraine would seem more likely.

Whatever it was, it hurt, humiliated, and limited Paul. At first he viewed it as a restrictive handicap, but when he saw it in its true perspective, he came to regard it as a heavenly advantage. God does not spare even His chosen servants acute suffering at times, but He also imparts the power to rise above it.

Because Paul regarded this thorn as a tormenting hindrance to his ministry, he pleaded for its removal on three occasions (2 Corinthians 12:8). He did not stop to inquire why it was there—he only wanted it to depart permanently. His was no desultory request, but a deep heart-cry, for his malady was tormenting him. He acted as though it was purposeless pain. He had yet to learn that God never acts out of caprice, and that no pain is purposeless.

Now Paul was face to face with the problem of unanswered prayer. Was God unsympathetic toward his suffering and his plea? But although God did not answer the specific words of Paul's prayer, He did respond to the cry of his heart. Paul's deep desire was that his ministry would not be hindered. God responded by assuring him that his ministry would be enriched if the thorn remained.

I prayed, the thorn remained,
But strength was perfected.

St. Augustine's mother prayed passionately that her profligate son might not go to Rome, which was a moral cesspool, lest he drift further into sin. Her specific prayer was unanswered. Yet Augustine's journey to Rome proved to be the first step to Milan where he was apprehended by the Lord. This is sometimes His method.

We ask for strength that we might achieve;
We are made weak that we might obey.
We ask for health that we may do greater things;
We are given infirmity that we may do things better.
We ask for power that we may win the praise of men;
We are given weakness that we may feel our need of
    God.
We ask for things that we may enjoy life;
We are given life that we may enjoy all things.
                                        ANONYMOUS

A Divine Gift

"There was given me a thorn in my flesh, *a messenger of Satan,* to torment me" (2 CORINTHIANS 12:7, emphasis added).

Paul does not say "there was *imposed* on me a thorn," but "there was *given* to me a thorn." The question arises, can a messenger of Satan be at the same time a gift from God? In this connection Margaret Clarkson writes:

> It is true that our pain comes to us only as God allows it. In this sense, and in this sense only, He may be said to "give" it. But suffering originates with Satan. It entered man's life only after his sin. It is part of sin's curse under which we must live until Christ sets up His righteous Kingdom.

It was not God who instituted this test, but apparently, as in the case of Job, He permitted Satan to sift His servant. To God, the spiritual welfare and growth of His children are of far greater importance than their temporal comfort. "God disciplines us for our good, that we may share in his holiness" (Hebrews 12:10). He is not the direct but the indirect source of our testing.

Note that Paul did not manufacture his own thorn. We are not called on to become spiritual fakirs, making beds of spikes for ourselves, as some are inclined to do. It will be time enough to embrace our thorn if and when God permits it to come to us.

Dr. Paul White, widely known as the Jungle Doctor, wrote in a letter:

> One of the most uncomfortable and most valuable things in my life since early childhood has been *Asthma*. Suffering a chronic disease is the best way to help anyone understand, think with and work for those with disabilities. *Suffering Matters. Turn your disabilities into opportunities.*

And he did just that.

Once Paul grasped the divine purpose in the trial, he never again prayed for its removal. His whole attitude changed. What transformed this importunate supplicant into a submissive sufferer? *An encounter with God.*

> "He said to me, 'My grace is sufficient for you, for my power is made perfect in weakness'" (2 CORINTHIANS 12:9).

Paul gave God a chance to speak to him, and when the voice of God distilled on his troubled heart, the tumult died. He embraced the will of God with a song, not a sigh.

What Is Your Thorn?

Is the memory of past failure haunting you? Most who have made anything have had failures, and God forgives these on repentance and confession (1 John 1:9).

Is it a tendency to depression, or some psychological ailment, or some physical infirmity? Paul suffered from this. In *The Acts of Hecla,* this description is given of him (although its authenticity cannot be vouched for). "A little man, going bald on top, crooked in the legs, with eyebrows joining and a hooked nose—and also full of grace."

Is it an unhappy marriage, or occupational pressures? Insoluble church or mission problems? Note and emulate Paul's attitude:

> "I will boast all the more gladly about my weaknesses so that Christ's power may rest on me. That is why, for Christ's sake I delight in weaknesses, in insults, in hardships, in persecutions, in difficulties. For when I am weak, then I am strong" (2 CORINTHIANS 12:9, 10).

The thorn had lost none of its sharpness, nor had the buffeting been any less severe, but the compensating grace of God had enabled Paul to turn the doleful dirge into a song of triumph.

> *Turn your trouble into treasure,*
> *Turn your sorrow into song.*
> *Then the world will know the measure*
> *In which you to Christ belong.*
>
> CATHERINE BOOTH

The world's philosophy is, "What can't be cured must be endured." But Paul's radiant testimony is, "What can't be cured can be enjoyed." "I even enjoy weakness, sufferings, hardships, and difficulties"—not for their own sake, but for the compensations they brought. But he constantly drew upon God's "more than sufficient grace." He was thus able to exchange his human weakness for divine power. God's power did not dispel the weakness, but it was *perfected* in it.

So, instead of pleading his suffering pain as an excuse for avoiding sacrificial service, or asking for its removal, Paul now laid hold on the power and grace of God, and attempted greater things for Him. He turned Satan's weapon against him and gained a glorious victory.

In this way the rapturous paradise experience paled before the glorious compensations of the painful thorn. In this trial, he exhibited "the mind of Christ."

CHAPTER 3

Transformation of the Mind

*"Do not conform any longer to the pattern
of this world, but be transformed by the renewing
of your mind" (ROMANS 12:2).*

*"Let this mind be in you, which was also in
Christ Jesus" (PHILIPPIANS 2:5, KJV).*

The natural mind, because of its inherited bias toward sin, is hostile to God and does not submit to His laws (Romans 8:7). Man's mind is therefore the battleground on which every moral and spiritual battle is fought. In the end, a person's mind-set determines his or her behavior.

Paul recognized this fatal disability, and so his counsel to the Roman Christians was the verse at the head of this chapter. He himself made it his objective to "take captive every thought to make it obedient to Christ" (2 Corinthians 10:5). It should be our objective to have our minds so completely transformed that we will accurately reflect the mind and attitude of Christ.

This will mean that in increasing measure we will think as He thinks, love as He loves, and value persons and things as He values them.

In the second verse at the head of the chapter, Paul throws out a tremendous challenge, which he reinforces with what is perhaps the greatest Christological statement in the New Testament.

Different translators have seen different facets of truth in the passage. Here are some:

> "Reflect in your minds the mind of Christ Jesus" (J. B. LIGHTFOOT).

> "Your attitude should be the same as that of Christ Jesus" (NIV).

> "Let the governing impulse of your life be the same as that of Christ Jesus" (W. W. CASH).

While we can never duplicate the mind of Christ, we can display the same attitude. We should therefore "cherish the disposition which was in Christ Jesus."

So then, the mind of Christ was His mindset, His whole inner disposition—His thoughts, desires, and motives, the governing impulse of His life. Paul urges us by prayer, diligent Bible study, and disciplined obedience to pursue inward likeness to Him.

Why the Disparity?

Why is it that we Christians make so slight an impact on our cynical and materialistic world? Is it not because we display so little of the mind and disposition of Christ? Stuart Holden suggested that the world does not believe in Him whom they have not seen because it has cause not to believe in us whom it has seen! They appear to see so little in our lives that would make it worth their while sacrificing what they already have.

Only the manifestation of the winsome, otherworldly Christ-mind in its utter contrast to the natural, earthly mind will convince others that we have something worthy of the sacrifice of all else.

This remarkable passage—Philippians 2:5–11—discloses that the Christ-mind expressed itself in a similar fashion in both His pre-incarnate and incarnate states. It was manifested on two planes.

The Plane of Deity

"Who, being in very nature God, did not consider equality with God something to be grasped, but made himself nothing, taking the very nature of a servant" (PHILIPPIANS 2:6).

The expression used here refers to essential attributes, not mere external appearance; not to superficial likeness, but to essential Godhead.

In His pre-incarnate state, He did not consider equality with God, with all its attendant majesty, a thing to be grasped and held on to at all costs. Instead, He made Himself nothing.

In His incarnate state, by a sublime act of self-surrender to His Father, He resigned His glories, veiled His majesty, and assumed the sinless limitations of humanity so that He could become the Mediator between God and man (1 Timothy 2:5).

There is no suggestion that in this self-emptying He laid aside His deity or divine attributes—only the independent exercise of them. The "emptying" is specifically limited to His "taking the very nature of a servant." (Note that it was not an exchange but an addition.) Conscious as He was of His place in the Godhead with the Father, He could never be other than God. But there were some things He could and would renounce. While He was not stripped of divine powers, He determined not to use them. As Bengel put it, "He remained full, but bore Himself as though He were empty." Instead of a sovereign, He became a servant. He exchanged His royal robes for a carpenter's smock, but He was still the same royal Person. He renounced the outward display of His majesty, and the privileges as well. John Milton fittingly described His descent.

That glorious form, that light insufferable,
And that far-beaming blaze of majesty
Wherewith He wont, at heaven's high council table
To sit the midst of Trinal unity,
He laid aside; and here with us to be,
Forsook the courts of everlasting day,
And chose with us a darksome house of mortal clay.

The Plane of Humanity

". . . being made in human likeness. And being found in appearance as a man, he humbled himself, and became obedient to death—even death on a cross!" (PHILIPPIANS 2:7–8).

What greater humiliation could humanity have heaped on Him? The Romans considered crucifixion so degrading that they would not permit a Roman to be crucified. The Jews considered one who was crucified to be under the curse of God.

In connection with our Lord's humiliation, it has been pointed out that every downward step He took would have permitted some amelioration without affecting the validity of His mediatorial work. He need not have been born in a manger; He could have been born in a palace. He could have attended a university instead of a village school. He could have come as a conquering hero instead of being despised and rejected by men.

He deliberately chose the lowest place, to demonstrate the mindset He expected in His disciples. We, in our turn, are to reflect the mind that brought the eternal Son of God down from a throne of glory to a cross of shame. But He proved that the Mount of Exaltation was as high as the Valley of Humiliation was deep!

> "Therefore God exalted him to the highest place and gave him the name that is above every name, that at the name of Jesus every knee should bow" (PHILIPPIANS 2:9–10)

God super-exalted Him to the throne of the universe. All that Christ had laid aside was restored to Him. He was not a permanent loser.

> *The highest place that heaven affords*
> *Is His by sovereign right;*
> *As King of kings and Lord of lords,*
> *He reigns in glory bright.*

The Christ-Mind Progressive

Our Lord's display of His mind was progressive. It began with "considering" (v. 6). It led to self-abasement (v. 8). It culminated in self-oblation (v. 8).

We might understandably say, "But He was the sinless Son of God. I am a sinful man, a sinful woman." It is true He had no sinful nature to contend with. But did He not say, "I have set you an example that you should do as I have done for you" (John 13:15)? While we cannot duplicate Christ's actions, we can in increasing measure display the same attitude.

For our encouragement, Scripture records how two men with sinful natures like ours demonstrated the mind of Christ in testing circumstances, Both Moses and Paul, though separated by centuries, manifested Christ-like attitudes.

Considering

Christ "did not consider equality with God something to be grasped" (v. 6).

Moses "regarded disgrace for the sake of Christ as of greater value than the treasures of Egypt" (Hebrews 11:26).

Paul said, "I consider everything a loss compared to the surpassing greatness of knowing Christ Jesus my Lord" (Philippians 3:8). The very things in which he formerly took pride, he now counted loss for Christ.

This was their deliberate mindset, and all that followed in their lives sprang from this studied attitude. They did not cling avidly to their rights, but gladly renounced them in the interests of the Kingdom.

Self-abasement

"*[Christ,]* being found in appearance as a man, he humbled himself" to take the very nature of a servant.

Note that His humiliation did not consist in *doing* the *work* of a servant. How complete was His identification with us men and women!

Moses humbled himself, choosing "to be mistreated along with the people of God rather than to enjoy the pleasures of sin for a short time" (Hebrews 11:25).

Paul delighted in his role as a "bondslave of Jesus Christ." He chose to renounce his equality with the theologians and philosophers of his day, and lived among men and women of every class.

Self-oblation

Christ chose "death—even death on a cross," that a lost humanity might be redeemed.

Moses, in self-forgetful love, prayed, "Oh, what a great sin these people have committed! They have made themselves gods of gold. But now, please forgive their sin—but if not, then blot me out of the book you have written" (Exodus 32:31, 32).

Paul, in the desperation of his love for his nation, wrote: "I have great sorrow and unceasing anguish in my heart. For I could wish that I myself were cursed and cut off from Christ for the sake of my brothers, those of my own race" (Romans 9:2, 3).

These passages of Scripture portray a practical demonstration of the mind of Christ in men of like passions as ourselves. Let us emulate them, remembering that they had no resources that are not equally available to us.

The Earthly Mind

So that we may more clearly grasp the governing impulse of our Lord's life, consider His attitude toward things cherished by most men and women.

Position and Power

The earthly mind covets and clutches these, and will go to great lengths to attain them. Even in religious circles there is sometimes an unseemly jockeying for position and power—an attitude entirely alien to the mind of Christ, who renounced pomp and power. He allowed His creatures to sneer, "Is not this the carpenter's son?"

To the earthly mind, wealth is the *summum bonum* of existence, to be gained at all costs, even if someone else goes to the wall in the process. Witness the way in which lucrative businesses and professions are crowded, while important work for Christ and humanity languishes for workers. When one influential pulpit in the United States fell vacant, there were 250 applicants!

How unlike the mind of Christ: "for [our] sakes he became poor so that [we] through his poverty might become rich" (2 Corinthians 8:9).

Service and Sacrifice

It is characteristic of the earthly mind that it usually covets the service of others. It desires to avoid toil and drudgery. That is one of the reasons why money is so desirable—it can secure the service of others.

What was Christ's mindset in this regard? "The Son of Man did not come to be served, but to serve" (Mark 10:45). "I am among you as one who serves" (Luke 22:27).

Samuel Logan Brengle was a brilliant student, the selected orator of his university. Upon graduation, he was called to the pulpit of an influential church in an American city, where he was acclaimed as a coming pulpiteer. Everything was going well, but his heart was not satisfied. He did not feel that he was reaching the people, and he longed to do more for the spread of the Gospel.

At this crucial juncture he read of the Salvation Army, which was then regarded as a rather disreputable organization. But as he read of its achievements in Britain among underprivileged people, and of the trophies it was winning from the gutter, he felt this was the type of work that would satisfy his yearning.

He resigned from his church and went to Britain, where he offered his services to General Booth. He was ultimately accepted for service, but in order to test his caliber, he was sent to the training garrison with cadets who, though full of zeal, were innocent of formal education.

One day he was assigned to clean a pile of muddy boots that belonged to fellow-students. It is not difficult to imagine the battle royal that was raging in his mind as he brushed away the mud. Was it for this that he had renounced his prestigious church? The devil pressed the advantage he had gained, and Brengle had almost succumbed to the tempter's voice. when a verse of Scripture was injected into his mind by the Holy Spirit: *"[He] wrapped a towel around his waist . . . and began to wash his disciples' feet."*

In a moment he detected the trail of the serpent, and from his heart he cried, "Lord, if you could take a towel and wash the disciples' dirty feet, surely I can take a brush and clean the cadets' dirty boots."

Humility triumphed—he chose the role of the servant. This victory laid a foundation for a life of service that multiplied itself a thousandfold in a worldwide ministry of revival.

Do we evidence the mind of Christ in this respect? Most want to be leaders. Few long to be servants. The many are usually served by the few.

Suffering and Shame

The earthly mind shrinks from suffering, or anything that would involve loss of face. But Christ actually courted these if blessing would accrue to others. He welcomed death as a criminal on an agonizing cross—the quintessence of suffering and shame. "I have a baptism to undergo," He said, "and how distressed I am until it is completed" (Luke 12:50). "Shall I not drink the cup the Father has given me?" (John 18:11).

The Christ-mind is so essentially opposed to the earthly mind that nothing less than a complete transformation is needed. Where did that mind lead Jesus? To the cross. If we allow the Holy Spirit to work that mind in us, where will it lead us? Just as inevitably to the cross, for nothing but the cross of Christ is sufficiently potent to work this transformation.

Much of Christianity today is crossless. The offense of the cross has ceased. No longer does it cut deeply into our way of life. As with the Greeks in our Lord's day, the current watchwords and philosophy of today are *self-culture and self-enjoyment.* The mind of Christ involves self-sacrifice and self-oblation, notes that are too often absent from the harmony of our lives.

The single grain of wheat that fell into the ground and died at Calvary (John 12:24) germinated and lived again in 3000 lives on the Day of Pentecost, and in millions of lives since then.

How are we to attain or obtain the mind of Christ? Can we generate it from within? Who could imitate and reproduce the grand, majestic, crystal-pure life of Christ? Who could imitate a Raphael?

Is not the secret hinted at in the exhortation: *"Let* this mind be in you"? It is the work of Another. Is not the supreme work of the Holy Spirit to reproduce in the life of the yielded believer the inner disposition of Christ? What is the fruit of the Spirit but the mind of Christ (Galatians 5:22, 23)?

As we purposefully yield to the sanctifying influences of the Holy Spirit, He will perform the miracle of a daily progress in Christlikeness. Our minds will be transformed in ever-increasing degree by His renewal.

So, let us heed Peter's exhortation: "Arm yourselves . . . with the same mind" (1 Peter 4:1, KJV).

CHAPTER 4

The Joy of a Clear Conscience

*"I strive always to keep my conscience clear
before God and man" (ACTS 24:16).*

Although the word *conscience* does not appear in the Old
Testament, the idea is prevalent from the time Adam
and Eve hid from God. It is surprising that Jesus never used the
word, although His teaching made a continuous appeal to the
conscience. It is used most frequently by Paul, but even he does
not clearly define it. The part it plays in human life can be
gauged by the fact that Shakespeare refers to it in thirty-one
world-famous passages.

The question arises, Is conscience a separate faculty of man's
moral nature? Is it a fallible human mechanism or an infallible
divine endowment?

From a consideration of the relevant Scriptures it appears to
be a special activity of the intellect and emotions that enables
one to judge between good and evil, to perceive moral distinctions. It has been defined as the testimony and judgment of the
soul that gives approbation or disapproval to the acts of the
will. As animals do not possess this capacity, they are incapable
of sin. Without it, man too could not be held responsible for sin
he was incapable of discerning. *It is the activity of conscience that
makes sin culpable.*

The word signifies "a knowledge held in conjunction with another"—in this instance, God. It carries the idea of man being co-witness with God for or against himself, according to his own estimate of his actions.

The philosopher Kant refers to it as "the categorical imperative." Conscience is the nerve center of the soul, sensitive to moral pleasure and pain. Its function is to adjudicate on the moral quality of an action, and how we should act in view of it.

Ignorance of the function of conscience and of God's provision for its healthy exercise can lead to serious spiritual disorders. Many sensitive Christians have limped through life because of a morbid and weak conscience, whose condemning voice allows them no respite.

Their very sincerity and desire to be obedient to the will of God has accentuated the problem and caused them to live in a state of self-accusation. Deliverance from this unhappy state is possible through the apprehension and appropriation of Scripture teaching on the subject. As Jesus said, truth is always potent to set us free.

The Nature of Conscience

Conscience is part of our essential nature, not something we gradually acquire. It is neither supernatural nor divine, but purely human equipment. It is often described as the voice of God in the soul, but if this were true, it could never lead to sinful action. Indeed, it may actually be the voice of the devil! It is not the voice of God, but rather the power to hear the voice of God in the soul.

Conscience originates nothing. Like a thermometer, which detects and indicates the temperature, yet never modifies or creates its own temperature, so it is with conscience. It is the highest and most mysterious faculty in the moral nature of man, and speaks with most convincing authority when habitually obeyed. When we obey it, we live in the Beatitudes. When we disobey it, like John the Baptist, it cries, "It is not lawful" (Matthew 14:4).

Paul assures us that pagans are endowed with conscience. They have a law within themselves that urges them to take a certain course of action, or to desist from it. A Canadian Indian picturesquely described the activity of his conscience: "It is a little three-cornered thing inside of me. When I do wrong it turns round and hurts me very much. But if I keep on doing wrong, it will turn so much that the corners become worn off and it doesn't hurt anymore."

With characteristic spiritual insight, John Bunyan in his *Holy War* represents the human family under the figure of a city. Mansoul. One of its citizens he calls Mr. Conscience. When Diabolus captured the city, he sought to destroy all traces of its former ownership by Emmanuel. Since he could not kill Mr. Conscience, he sought to imprison him in a deep dungeon where his voice would be effectively silenced.

But when Emmanuel undertook the recapture of Mansoul, as soon as veteran Captain Conviction led the assault against Ear Gate, old Mr. Conscience was so aroused that he began to shout in his dungeon until the whole city was stirred at his voice, loudly calling for their allegiance to Emmanuel and condemning the rebellion against his authority.

It must be noted that *conscience is not an executive faculty.* It has no power to make a person do right or cease to do wrong. It delivers its judgment, produces the appropriate emotion, but leaves it to the will to act in the light of its verdict. It has no further responsibility (Romans 2:15).

Limitations of Conscience

"I live by my conscience" is the complacent statement sometimes made, as though that rendered the resulting action right. But is conscience an infallible guide? By no means. "My conscience is clear," said Paul, "but that does not make me innocent" (1 Corinthians 4:4). It cannot therefore be infallible, but is a fluctuating factor reacting faithfully to the standard of moral conduct to which it witnesses. That standard may be imperfect or even flagrantly wrong, but such as it is, conscience will adjudicate according to it.

In former times the conscience of a Hindu would protest loudly against the killing of a cow, but would remain quiescent while he sacrificed his child. A Hindu once said to a British administrator, "Our conscience tells us it is right to burn our widows on the pyre of their husbands." "Yes," replied the administrator, "and our conscience tells us it is right to hang you if you do." It is all a matter of the moral standard to which conscience witnesses. If the standard accepted is a wrong one, conscience will allow such horrors as the Inquisition in the name of Christ.

The fact is that every conscience needs instruction. Its delicate mechanism has been thrown off balance by the Fall. Just as a bullet will reach the bull's-eye only if the two sights are in correct alignment, so correct moral judgments are delivered only when conscience is correctly aligned with the Scriptures. And herein lies a powerful argument for the reverent and diligent study of the whole Word of God.

Just as a watch must be set and regulated by standard time, so conscience must be set and regulated by God's infallible standard as revealed in His Word. And of course, the only norm of character is our Lord Jesus Christ. If we walk with Him, our standards will be ever rising.

While conscience responds obediently to the standard of right that it knows, it is limited by habit and prejudice. These can speak so loudly that they seem to be the very voice of conscience. So blinded with prejudice and bigotry was Paul that he thought he was obeying the voice of God in persecuting the church. Often when we think we are standing for principle, we are only falling for prejudice.

So then a conscience regulated by the Word of God is the monitor of the soul, which insists on right doing, condemns wrongdoing, produces remorse when flouted, and imparts peace when heeded (Acts 24:16).

A Condemning Conscience

Conscience either commends or condemns any purposed action, and Scripture lists four progressive states in each category. First consider the possible states of the condemning conscience which "makes cowards of us all."

A weak conscience is one that is not healthy but morbid, overscrupulous, and oversensitive (1 Corinthians 8:7–12). It reacts faithfully according to its light, but like a compass with a weak magnetic current, it is easily influenced and tends to vacillate. Its possessor is constantly tormented by doubt as to whether an action is right or wrong. It constantly digs up in unbelief what has been sown in faith.

A conscience may be weak for two reasons—an imperfect knowledge of God's Word and will, with a consequent imperfect faith, or an unsurrendered will that gives a vacillating choice. Anyone who obeys God's revealed will, or is willing to do that will, need not be harassed by an overscrupulous conscience. We should resolutely refuse to constantly review an action committed in good faith. Those with weak consciences are given to the unsatisfying occupation of photographing themselves and developing the films. The corrective is to face the issues involved in a situation in the light of Scripture, seek the guidance of the Spirit, and come to a decision according to one's best judgment. Thereafter refuse to reopen the matter.

A defiled conscience may degenerate from a weak one. Its very weakness makes it more susceptible to defilement. Paul affirms this: "Some people are still so accustomed to idols that when they eat such food they think of it as having been sacrificed to an idol, and since their conscience is *weak*, it is *defiled*" (1 Corinthians 8:7, emphasis added).

If we persist in some action against which conscience has protested, we thereby defile it and prevent its faithful functioning. A little dust can derange the delicate mechanism of a watch. So with conscience. "To the pure, all things are pure, but to those who are corrupted . . . nothing is pure. In fact, both their minds and consciences are corrupted" (Titus 1:15).

An evil or guilty conscience (Hebrews 10:22) results from habitual defilement. If its possessor will practice evil, then it will permit him or her to do it with less and less remonstrance. It begins to react to their lowering standards, until it comes to regard evil as good and good as evil. A burglar who was guilty of every crime imaginable, and whose conscience had never troubled him over his crimes, was filled with remorse because he had spent $10 entrusted to him by another burglar!

A seared or cauterized conscience is the ultimate condition of one who has habitually defied its verdict. It is reduced to insensitivity and no longer protests. "Such teachings come through hypocritical liars whose consciences have been seared as with a hot iron" (1 Timothy 10:2). This is a terrible condition. No appeal will succeed, for it has been done to death.

Vice is a monster of such frightful mien
That to be hated, needs but to be seen;
But seen too oft, familiar with her face,
We first endure, then pity, then embrace.

ALEXANDER POPE

Note the downward progress. A pure conscience becomes weak and defiled, But it will not remain long at this stage unless its purity is restored by renouncing of the evil and appropriating the cleansing God offers. It deteriorates and becomes evil, permitting its possessor to practice wrong without remonstrance. The claim, "My conscience did not trouble me," is more likely to betoken an evil than a pure conscience. Then comes the final condition—seared. With relief we turn to

A Commending Conscience

This is a prize to be coveted above all else. "Dear friends, if our hearts [consciences] do not condemn us, we have confidence before God" (1 John 3:21). Conscience is just as faithful in commending for the right as in condemning for the wrong.

A pure conscience (2 Timothy 1:3) is one which, doing its duty faithfully, is very sensitive to the approach of evil. It is the mind's alarm clock, set to go off at its approach. A proprietor of stables for horses purchased a load of straw from a menagerie. His horses became restless and uneasy. Although they had never seen a lion, they sensed that their natural enemy had been in contact with the straw. Conscience is kept pure and sensitive as we obey the light shed on our conduct by the Scriptures. It reacts to that standard and will accept nothing short of it. "Deacons . . . must keep hold of the deep truths of the faith with a clear conscience. . ." (1 Timothy 3:8–9).

A good conscience is the happy possession of the person who in all things accepts the dictates of the pure conscience (1 Timothy 1:5, 19). Its reproof is welcomed and acted on by eliminating what is wrong and adding what is deficient. This brings serenity and heart rest. Peace of conscience is not an accident but an acquisition. It is not a matter of temperament but of attainment.

A Cleansed Conscience

The conscience has no panacea for its own ills, but Scripture indicates that a twofold cleansing is necessary and possible.

"Since we have these promises... let us purify ourselves from everything that contaminates body and spirit" (2 Corinthians 7:1) is the divine injunction. The first step in restoring purity of conscience is, by a definite act of the will and in reliance on the Holy Spirit, to separate ourselves from all we know to be sinful and contrary to God's will. If we are unwilling to do this, we disqualify ourselves from experiencing the cleansing of the blood of Christ. But if we resolutely deal with sin, the Holy Spirit will confirm us in our purpose and enable its achievement.

This cleansing, purifying of ourselves—separating ourselves from all known sin—is only a necessary preparation for conscience being "cleansed by the blood of Christ."

The infallible prescription is given in Hebrews 9:7–14.

"The blood of goats and bulls and the ashes of a heifer sprinkled on those who are ceremonially unclean sanctify them so that they are outwardly clean. How much more, then, will the blood of Christ... cleanse our consciences from acts that lead to death."

The characteristic of the sacrifice of the red heifer, alluded to in this passage, was that it was always readily available and accessible. So with the cleansing of the blood of Christ. But as with the conscience-stricken Israelite, so with us: the available sacrifice must be personally appropriated.

> *Precious, precious blood of Jesus,*
> *Ever flowing free,*
> *I believe it, I receive it,*
> *'Tis for me.*

The forgiveness of the worst sin causes it to pass immediately and completely from the conscience. Never again need it haunt us. Conscience, like a released spring, returns to its normal action of warning against the fresh approach of sin and adjudicating on the character of moral action. The Holy Spirit, who applies the powerful solvent of the blood of Christ to the defiled conscience in response to faith, delights to make it possible for us to live with a conscience "void of offense toward God and man."

CHAPTER 5

Is God Fair?

"The house of Israel says, 'The way of the Lord is not just'"(Ezekiel 18:29).

"If I want him to remain alive until I return, what is that to you? You must follow me" (John 21:22).

Some of God's dealings with His children seem to run contrary to our innate sense of what is fair, and tested saints in all ages have been tempted to complain with Israel, "The way of the Lord is not just." Some of our contemporaries seem to enjoy preferential treatment, and instead of faithfully discharging our responsibilities, we look over our shoulders at others.

This was a tendency of Peter with which Jesus dealt very faithfully on two occasions. At times there seemed to be a touch of acerbity in the Lord's response to Peter's inappropriate statements, and we may be inclined to feel that the fisherman received more than his share of rebuffs at the hand of Him who was meekness and love incarnate.

Surely his well-intentioned suggestion that the Master might be a little easier on Himself hardly merited the sharp rebuke: "Get behind me Satan! You are a stumbling block to me; you do not have in mind the things of God, but the things of men" (Matthew 16:23). And did not his innocuous inquiry about John's future—"Lord, what about him?"—meet with an unnecessarily sharp answer—"What is that to *you?*" (John 21:21, 22, emphasis added). A polite way of saying, "Peter, mind your own business."

Did the Lord take pleasure in baiting him, or was He teaching him important truths he would learn in no other way? Undoubtedly, one underlying reason for the sternness of the Lord's words has relevance for all His servants today. Jesus had just concluded His tender yet soul-searching interview with the now humbled and penitent Peter. In response to the Master's thrice-repeated question, he had made a renewed protestation of love, and had received a fresh commission. Then the Lord gave a prophetic intonation of the violent death by which he would glorify God (John 21:15–19).

An Irrelevant Question

One would have thought that the moving experiences of the last few hours would have sufficed to concentrate Peter's attention on the interests of the Master who had so graciously restored and recommissioned him. But no! Instead, he begins comparing his future with that of John. Immediately his mind flies off at a tangent and his ever-ready tongue blurts out: "Lord, what about him?" In His customary manner Jesus answered Peter's captious question with another: "If I want him to remain alive until I return, what is that to you? You must follow me" (John 21: 22).

Peter was intruding into a realm that was no concern of his. In the shock of learning that he would have to tread the pathway of rejection and suffering, his first reaction was to compare his lot with that of others. Is he being discriminated against? Will John be bound and led where he doesn't want to go, or will he receive preferential treatment (John 21:18)? Peter took his eyes off his Master and fixed them on John.

In Peter's question it is not difficult to discern the rise of a new self-pity. But instead of answering his querulous question, Jesus rebuked his curiosity: "What is that to you? You must follow me." He who had just asserted his right to determine and reveal Peter's future, now asserts His rights over John (v. 22).

Subsequent events revealed that Peter was being trained in the school of Christ, in order to equip him for a supremely important role in His Kingdom, and he must learn his lessons thoroughly. In following his Lord he must never turn about and compare his lot with that of another disciple.

Peter's constant temptation was to try to manage other people's affairs. Did he not on one occasion even try to manage Jesus (Matthew 16:22)? He must learn that his Master deals with each of us disciples individually, and in ways that are not always clear or explicable to others. Did Peter but know it, John's would be no path of roses. He would drink of the cup of suffering as deeply as he, but that was no concern of Peter's. His sole care was to follow his Lord, watching his own walk, and discharging his responsibility to feed the flock of God (John 21:15–17).

Note that Jesus offered no explanation or interpretation of His rebuke, for the sovereign Lord is under no obligation to explain Himself to His disciple. He simply made it crystal clear that Peter was meddling in a matter that was no concern of his. Jesus offered no word of comfort, but to administer comfort at this juncture would be to induce self-pity and indulge weakness. Peter was a soldier engaged in relentless warfare, and he must have rigorous training. Here then is the background reason for the stern rebuke. Jesus needs heroes, not meddlers. He must have those who, without self-pity, render unquestioning obedience to His command.

The Master gives no quarter even to natural and temperamental weakness. He allows Peter to smart under the rebuke, for he is engaged in total warfare. He does not even correct his mistaken assumption that John would not die.

Earlier Peter had shown the same tendency. The rich young ruler, possessed by his possessions, had rejected Christ's call to follow Him and had gone away sorrowful. Explaining the moral, Jesus remarked on the difficulty with which a rich man entered the kingdom of God. The ever-ready Peter, with conscious superiority over the young ruler, interposed with, "We have left everything to follow you! What then will there be for us?" (Matthew 19:16–30).

He doubtless expected that superior loyalty and devotion would gain precedence at the last day. And he was not mistaken! Jesus assured him that those who had sacrificially followed Him would receive a hundred times as much, and inherit eternal life. But He added a solemn rider: "But many who are first will be last, and many who are last will be first." Peter must not compare himself favorably with the young ruler, but scrutinize his *own* motivation.

Motive and Recompence

The motive behind the renunciation was all-important. Peter's question was very revealing. "We have left everything. *What will there be for us?*" (emphasis added). The motive that would receive the hundredfold recompense is stated in v. 29— *"for my sake."* When our paramount motive in service is that we might get something, we miss that for which we aim. But when our motive is love for Christ, He is careful to see that we are not losers—"a hundred times as much . . . eternal life."

The same principle emerges in the subsequent parable of the farmer who hired laborers to work in his vineyard. When those who had been engaged at daybreak saw the latecomers who had been engaged at 5:00 in the afternoon receive the same remu-neration as they themselves, they began to feel cheated (Matthew 20:1–16).

True, they had received the wage agreed on—and a fair wage too—but were they being treated fairly? When they voiced their complaint, the farmer met them with two unanswerable propositions. First, "Friend, I am not being unfair to you. Didn't you agree to work for a denarius?" He had not defrauded them; he had fulfilled his contract. From the standpoint of justice they had no case. Second, "Don't I have the right to do what I want with my own money? Or are you envious because I am generous?" His generosity hurt no one but himself.

The reward was not according to the length of time worked, but according to the faithful use of the opportunity granted. The trouble with the twelve-hour workers is evident in their unwar-ranted complaints: "they expected to receive more," and "you have made them equal to us."

In this rather drastic way, Jesus made clear to Peter that He would not be dictated to concerning His dealings with His other disciples. He wrongs no one if He appears to be more generous or lenient with one than with another. That is His prerogative.

The personal application is not difficult to see. If the Lord seems to treat others with more generosity, bestowing on them what He withholds from us, if He permits the dark clouds of sorrow or suffering to shadow our lives while others bask in the sunshine, how are we to react?

We should remember that "Now we see but a poor reflec-tion as in a mirror. . . . Now [we] know [only] in part" (1 Corinthians 13:12). Things may be more equal than they now seem to our myopic vision. And then, who knows the hid-den grief and burden of another's heart?

Secret Ballast

When at the height of his well-deserved fame, David Livingstone the intrepid missionary-explorer said to an admiring well-wisher: "There is a kindly hand which behind the scenes applies the ballast, when to all appearances we are sailing gloriously with the wind." His secret ballast was an erring son who was causing him great sorrow.

We should accept it as axiomatic that God's dealings with our fellow disciples are no concern of ours. Our business is to watch our own motives carefully, to keep our eyes on the Lord, and not to look over our shoulders at others.

This principle has special relevance on the mission field as well as in the homeland, for the sins of envy and covetousness can thrive in either place. Do others receive large personal gifts, more lavish outfit and equipment? Do others appear to receive preferential treatment? Do we envy the more attractive personality or greater gifts of others? Do others seem less conscientious in the use of time or money, or in the conduct of their work? Has someone received promotion that we felt was our due? Do we experience more hardships or have fewer comforts than some others in the same circle? Do others enjoy success that is denied to us?

To each of these questions the Lord gives the same answer: *"What is that to you? You must keep on following me."*

It is not for us to fret over the Lord's treatment of another. We can rest assured that that person is being disciplined by the same loving hand, although in another way.

We can learn the blessedness that comes from finding no cause of stumbling in the Lord, or in the manner in which He disciplines others or ourselves (Matthew 11:6). We should cheerfully recognize and rejoice in the fact that others may do what we cannot, and enjoy what we have not. Our dealings must be directly with God. Our whole concern should be that we become like Caleb, a believer who "followed the LORD wholeheartedly" (Joshua 14:8).

CHAPTER 6

Tension and Stress—
Cause and Cure

"We do not want you to be uninformed, brothers,
about the hardships we suffered in the province of Asia.
We were under great pressure, far beyond our ability
to endure, so that we despaired even of life"
(2 CORINTHIANS 1:8).

Some degree of tension and stress is inherent in the human situation, but these conditions are more characteristic of our frenzied society than of any before. People in all walks of life are victims of their ravages, and in spite of the promises of heart-rest the Scriptures offer to the trusting soul, Christians are among the number affected.

By common consent, pastors, missionaries, and Christian workers are expected to know God and His ways better than the rank and file of believers, but they are by no means exempt from harmful stress and tension. Many seem unable to find release and enter into the "Sabbath-rest for the people of God" (Hebrews 4:9).

The word *tension* is defined as "the state of being strained to stiffness, hence mental strain, nervous anxiety with attending muscular stiffness." *Stress* is defined as "a force, acting on or within another thing, and tending to distort it, as by pulling or twisting it." Together, they combine to produce inability to relax, mental strain, and muscular tenseness.

Not all nervous tension is harmful. The string of a harp fulfills its function only as it attains the tension necessary to produce the correct musical note. So it is with the human life. Its highest achievement is reached only when every power is harnessed to the fulfillment of a worthy life purpose, and this involves a certain degree of tension. Fulfilling the will of His Father involved Jesus in tension. One rendering of Luke 12:50 is, "What tension I suffer until it is all over."

Stress is *excessive* tension, and it is with this that we are concerned.

Contributory Causes

It is a common misconception that it is hard work that generates tension, but work *per se* is not the real cause. When the mind is at rest, even hard work is health-giving. It produces fatigue, not tension. The fundamental cause of stress is usually to be found in the mind, not in the body.

I believe that four main factors induce stress and tension in the Christian worker.

A sense of inadequacy

A haunting consciousness of inadequate spiritual resources and mental acumen for one's tasks is a prolific cause of stress. And it is usually so well-based! Who of us is fully adequate for the responsibilities entrusted to us? With this conscious deficiency, the more conscientious we are, the more we strive and strain to supplement our lacks.

The perfectionist who has a highly developed sense of duty suffers most in this respect. A feeling that our spiritual capital is too meager to meet the heavy drafts being made on it tends to bring us to the breaking point.

An attitude of anxiety

The habit of worrying about things beyond our power to control can paralyze the nerve of spiritual endeavor and set up dangerous tensions, With some, this is a hereditary tendency that has come to be accepted as inevitable. The victim knows that it is futile and counterproductive, but feels powerless to break a habit that through long indulgence has become a life-pattern.

Examinations, health, affairs of the heart, language study, preparation of sermons and messages, difficult meetings or interviews, relations with colleagues—these constitute more sources of anxious care. The word Jesus used for "anxious care" signifies a dividing and distracting of the mind, so that it is kept in a state of agitation and is unable to give undivided attention to any one thing.

A condition of fear

This commonly generates stress. Some people of nervous temperament are afraid of everything. Fear of new responsibilities or of undertaking untried tasks fills the timid soul with an agony of apprehension. Physical fear, which in many cases is justified, can have far-reaching effects on both the nervous system and the spiritual life.

It can banish sleep, and fill even waking hours with a nameless feeling of dread. Fear of failure tends to produce the very condition it seeks to avoid, for God responds to faith, not fear. Fear and faith are mutually exclusive and cannot coexist in the same heart. The fear of man, fear of what people will think or say, brings with it not only a snare, but strain and stress (Proverbs 29:25).

A wrong attitude toward others

When we harbor an inner resentment against someone, even though almost unconsciously, it can work havoc with the nervous system. The cancer of jealousy, envy, or hatred will do the same. It was not without profound reason Paul exhorted that these destructive emotions be resolutely "put off," for they are not only sinful, but soul-destroying and health-wrecking as well.

When the pressures that descend on us from so many directions are added to one or all of these wrong attitudes and emotions, one's inner stress reaches the breaking point. On the mission field, lack of time for study, correspondence, reports, accounts and interviews, home duties and interruptions all add their quota of stress.

The continual pressure of crowds in home or clinic, whether they be concerned or only curious, deprives one of needed privacy and quiet. Add to these what Paul called, "the care of all the churches," the care for the spiritual welfare of your flock, and you have pressures before which the mind reels. Who can live in conditions such as these, especially in an energy-sapping climate, without stress and strain? We cry with Paul: "Who is sufficient for these things?"

Consequent Results

It does not require a physician to tell us that stresses of this sort will exact their toll from both body and spirit. And one uncomfortable quality of stress is that it is self-communicating. When we are under tension others know and feel it, and we are unable to impart spiritual lift to the atmosphere. It manifests itself in:

Physical disabilities

Stress and tension can produce nervous dyspepsia, which may have its source less in the food we eat than in the thoughts we think. The man on the street knows that there is a connection between ulcers and mental stress. Is not the increasing tendency to migraine and insomnia in our times, with a consequent addiction to the appropriate medications, merely the outraged nervous system taking its revenge on us for submitting it to strains God never meant it to carry? And may not some of our nervous disorders really be spiritual in origin?

Mental turmoil

Aware that unresolved inner tensions inevitably produce mental unrest and turmoil, the hymn writer prays, "I would not have the restless mind that hurries to and fro." The mind becomes unable to give undivided attention to the things of the Spirit because it is in a constant whirl.

During prayer times, thoughts become especially uncontrollable, swinging to the latest cause of concern as the needle to the pole. Even in sleep, the restlessness of the body reflects the deeper restlessness of the mind.

Spiritual depression

This is the logical climax. How could one but be depressed when body and mind form an alliance against the spirit? This condition affords our experienced and ruthless adversary a unique opportunity of exploiting his advantage with either a fiery dart or an oppressive cloud, as may best serve his purpose.

Thus the sensitive and hard-pressed soul is brought into spiritual bondage—haunted with a sense of defeat, and oppressed with the comparative lack of fruit in character and service.

Is There a Panacea?

Is there a way out of this prison-house, a real possibility of deliverance? Is it merely chasing a mirage to expect God, as the hymn puts it, to "Take from our lives the strain and stress,/ and let our ordered lives confess/ the beauty of Thy peace"?

There is a way of relief for those who are prepared to be ruthlessly honest with themselves and with God, and who are deeply in earnest in their search for the key to their problem. Taking the following steps could bring deliverance.

A rediscovery of God

We must begin with God, the Great Physician. Nothing less than a new discovery of God in all His power, love, and glory will meet the deepest need of our complex personalities. God Himself is the answer, and He will grant us the revelation of Himself when we are ready for what it involves. To the saints of past ages He granted a progressive revelation of Himself exactly suited to their pressing need. What we need is a fresh revelation of Him as *El Shaddai,* God All-Sufficient, immeasurably greater than our conscious inadequacy and need.

The trouble is that our God is too small, or rather that our conception and knowledge of God are too limited. We act as though He is inadequate to cope with the complexities and weaknesses of our natures. We must have a larger God. To magnify our insufficiency as we do, instead of laying hold of His abundant resources, is not only harmful but sinful. Did not Moses' harping on his insufficiency provoke God to anger (Exodus 4:14)? His attitude implied that God who had called him could not be trusted to supply him with the ability necessary to fulfill those responsibilities.

How can we discover a larger God? Through meditation on His Word—and this takes time and a fixed purpose. There is no easy shortcut. Read passages that magnify His greatness and power, such as Isaiah 40. Meditate on the way in which He changed the apostles after Pentecost. Ponder such assertions as those made in Ephesians 1:3; 2 Peter 1:3; 1 Corinthians 3:21. Believe in the availability of these resources and *appropriate* them. *Now.*

He who knows our need has made adequate provision for it, whether it is in the realm of the body, the mind, or the spirit. The disciples' lack of bread did not take Him by surprise or embarrass Him, for "he . . . knew what he would do" (John 6:6, KJV). He always does. To regain such a confidence in our great God cannot but relax the tensions, for they develop only when we have a God inadequate to meet our need.

A recognition of self

The villain of the piece, the center and source of stress, is self. When we recognize this, we are moving along the road to deliverance. Do we sometimes feel that more is asked of us, either by God or man, than we are able to bear? This may be true if we assume responsibilities not assigned by God. God will never overload us and He knows our load limit. He has given us the assurance that He will send no test that is beyond our ability to bear.

> "No temptation has seized you except what is common
> to man. And God is faithful; He will not let you be

tempted beyond what you can bear. But when you are tempted, He will also provide a way out so that you can stand up under it" (1 CORINTHIANS 10:13).

If, as the Scriptures teach and we profess to believe, there are no second causes, then we shall be able to do all that God commands. Jethro's words to Moses contain an unchanging principle:

"If you do this and God so commands, you will be able to stand the strain" (EXODUS 18:23).

Do we feel that there are not enough hours in the day for all we have to do? Jesus said, "Are there not twelve hours in the day?"—implying that for every God-assigned task there will be enough time to do it. It is more than probable that some of our too-numerous activities are self-imposed rather than divinely ordered, and should therefore be discontinued. Make a point of assessing your activities.

When we depreciate ourselves and our abilities, our insincerity sometimes shows through when someone else says the same things about us! Are we so often more anxious to secure the praise of men than the approval of God? And does not some of the stress arise from our endeavor to keep up spiritual appearances so that we may obtain it? We are prone to self-pity and are often vocally sorry for ourselves and our hard lot. Yet in His startling words to Peter, Jesus made it clear that self-pity was satanic in origin (Matthew 16:23).

Self is indeed the villain of the piece, and the real root of our trouble is that self has not abdicated the throne in favor of Christ. When His flag flies over the citadel of Mansoul, strain and stress give place to rest and serenity.

A renewal of mind

This is a third step on the path to deliverance. Permanent deliverance requires a radical change of attitude and a genuine renewal of mind.

At the conclusion of a conference at which I once spoke, a brilliant Indian woman said, "As a result of these meetings God has entirely reversed my thinking." Her mind was renewed and brought into harmony with the mind of Christ.

So long as the mental attitude remains unchanged, the tension and stress will continue. Instead of pitying and excusing ourselves because of the pressures under which we labor, we must view them no longer as amiable and unavoidable infirmities, but as culpable and unnecessary sins. We will see them not as a burden that crushes us but as a platform for the display of our God's sufficiency. We will hear Him say, "Now you will see what I will do" (Exodus 6:1). Now that we have got our eyes off ourselves and fixed on Him. The greater our weakness, the greater the glory that will accrue to God as we work in His power.

But how does this change of attitude, this renewal of mind, come? How can we induce it?

It will be the outcome of *a definite, purposeful choice of the will.* Do you *choose* to transfer the burden to Christ and leave it there? Do you *choose* to have done with anxiety and worry? Then hear what Paul says.

> "You were taught . . . to put off your old self, which is being corrupted by its deceitful desires; *to be made new in the attitude of your minds;* and to put on the new self, created to be like God" (EPHESIANS 4:22, 23, emphasis added).

"Be transformed by the renewing of your mind" (ROMANS 12:2).

This is obviously not something we can do ourselves, but something God will do in response to our faith. Paul says that this renewal is the work of the Holy Spirit (Titus 3:5).

When we are willing to stop excusing and exonerating ourselves for our condition, and cast ourselves wholly upon God, then the way is open for the Holy Spirit to work the miracle of renewing our minds. In other words, He will work in us the "mind . . . which was also in Christ Jesus" (Philippians 2:5, KJV) in increasing measure. That this would be a supernatural change is true, but then, is not Christianity a supernatural religion from beginning to end?

We may expect the Holy Spirit to make real to us the reinforcing presence of the Lord Jesus who dwells within us, to meet our daily and hourly needs, and remove stress and tension, replacing it with His peace. He promised,

> "Come to me, all you who are weary and burdened, and I will give you rest. Take my yoke upon you and learn from me . . . and you will find rest for your souls. For my yoke is easy and my burden is light" (MATTHEW 11:28–30).

Regular quietness and relaxation

These will make a valuable contribution on the physical plane. The psalmist counsels: "Be still, and know that I am God" (Psalm 46:10)"—a prescription we follow too seldom. "One of the ways in which man brings the most trouble upon himself is by his inability to be still," wrote Pascal.

We are busier than God intends us to be if we are too busy to take time for reasonable relaxation, and should adjust our agenda accordingly. The Lord constantly sought the stillness and solitude of the mountaintop. He impressed on His disciples the necessity of going apart for relaxation, and we disregard His counsel to our own loss. Let us covet the ability to move from one duty to another with a leisured heart.

One of God's gentlemen concluded his prayer with a self-revealing sentence: "And so, Lord, we move blithely into the new day." Blithely! No stress, no quivering tension—only a heart at rest in the God who is sufficient.

CHAPTER 7

No Handicapped Christians!

*"Therefore, there is now no condemnation for those
who are in Christ Jesus, because through Christ Jesus
the law of the spirit of life set me free from the law
of sin and death" (ROMANS 8:1–2).*

*I*n his book, *Christ's Slaves,* Archbishop Harrington C.
Lees has put us in his debt for an illuminating suggestion,
derived from the Greek papyri discovered in the early years of
this century:

> One of the great debts which we owe to the modern dis-
> coveries of those who have been translating for us the
> Greek papyri is this: that the word "no condemnation" has
> a different bearing to what we often thought. The word in
> Greek, though still a legal term, is not criminal but civil.
> It refers to land on which there is a legal embarrassment,
> a handicap, a mortgage, a restrictive covenant, a ground
> rent, some arrears; the dead hand of the past pressing
> upon the tenure of the present. The estate must be guar-
> anteed free from that. "No drawback," says the lawyer
> when he makes the conveyance and passes over the estate.

So long as there is an encumbrance of any kind on a property
or estate, the legal owner does not have free and unrestricted

enjoyment of his property, since someone else has a claim on it. But in the verse at the head of this chapter, Paul assures us that to those who are "in Christ Jesus," united to Him by a living faith, there is no sort of handicap, no sort of condemnation either civil or criminal to spoil the enjoyment of our inheritance.

Our disabilities and apparent handicaps need not limit our usefulness or spoil our enjoyment of the Christian life—this is the optimistic message of this passage. We are not doomed to limp along doing our poor best, hardly daring to hope that the future can be better than the past. There is provision in Christ and through the Holy Spirit for release and deliverance from our temperamental and psychological problems.

Nowhere in literature, sacred or profane, is there a more poignant portrayal of the defeated life than in Romans 7. The anguish of the heart that approves the good but falls prey to the evil is depicted with graphic strokes:

> "I do not understand what I do. For what I want to do
> I do not do, but what I hate I do" (v. 15).

The apostle is deeply conscious of an inversion of will. His whole will is against the involuntary sinful actions of the flesh. He does not consciously choose them, but when the crucial moment in temptation comes, his will is paralyzed. The nadir is reached in verse 24:

> "What a wretched man I am! Who will rescue me from
> this body of death?"

Then he emerges into the light. "Thanks be to God—through Jesus Christ our Lord!" (v. 25).

From the unrelieved pessimism of chapter 7, we progress into the infectious optimism of chapter 8, as though we were entering another world.

> "Therefore, there is now no condemnation [no handicap, no disability] for those who are in Christ Jesus" (PHILIPPIANS 8:1).

Some have difficulty in following Paul's argument as it moves out of chapter 7 into chapter 8. In chapter 5 Paul deals with deliverance from the penalty of sin. Chapter 6 represents sin as a tyrant from whose power the cross of Christ brings deliverance. Chapter 7 depicts in Technicolor the civil war in the believer's heart, which climaxes in the anguished cry for deliverance from the bondage and power of sin. But in chapter 8 it seems as though the argument swings back to deliverance from sin's condemnation and penalty. In reality, this is not the case.

With the fresh light from the papyri on the meaning of the word *condemnation*, it is not difficult to follow Paul's argument.

In chapter 7, the Christian is groaning under the pressure of past sin and failure that is cramping and blighting his present experience. The message of chapter 8 is that spiritual failure in the past need not adversely affect present experience, for "there is *now* no condemnation to those who are in Christ Jesus"—no handicap, no disability, no encumbrance (emphasis added). The only qualification is that we be "in Christ Jesus." Since this is the privilege of every true believer, it is true of us, no matter how we feel. We need no longer crawl along under the crippling handicaps and disabilities of the past. Nothing is carried over from the old life whose power has not been broken judicially through our union with Christ in His death and resurrection. This is the Gospel, the good news for the believer struggling against sin.

However, it is one thing to see a truth taught in Scripture, and quite another to translate it into daily personal experience in the context of our own temperament and environment. Is there some secret?

As we read chapter 7, we note that it is studded with the capital "I" and "me" —no fewer than forty times. The Holy Spirit is mentioned only twice. But in chapter 8, the capital "I" appears only once (and then in a joyous connection); the Holy Spirit is prominent—sixteen occurrences. This gives us a clue.

The open secret is that deliverance from the power and dominance of sin will be ours when the capital "I" ceases to hold the central place in our lives, and the Holy Spirit is honored and obeyed. He can then mediate to us the resurrection power of Christ. That is what Paul is saying in verse 2. "Through Christ Jesus the law of the Spirit of life has *set me free* from the law of sin and death" (emphasis added).

The Holy Spirit is the divine dynamic. More is said about Him in this chapter than anywhere else, except in the Upper Room discourse. It is He who transforms defeat and despair into victory and delight.

So this chapter presents the believer as free from the hampering shackles and encumbrances of the past and able to "walk in the Spirit." Not sinless, not infallible, but no longer haunted by the specter of past sin and failure. Paul's "no handicap, no disability" is good news indeed.

How glad we should be that our great high priest shared the sinless weaknesses of our human nature and is able to sympathize with our weaknesses (Hebrews 4:15). In the gift of the

Holy Spirit, He has made adequate provision for every handicap and drawback to which we are subject.

We shall now turn our attention to some of the very real handicaps to which this ministry of the Holy Spirit is the satisfying answer.

A Sinful Bias

"... the law of sin and death..." (ROMANS 9:2).

This law is universally operative, giving us a fatal bias toward sin. None of us has a natural tendency toward holiness. The hymn puts it accurately:

And every virtue we possess,
And every victory won,
And every thought of holiness,
Are His alone.

This verse highlights two opposing laws, the higher of which offsets and neutralizes the power of the lower. It is the power of the Holy Spirit that counteracts sin's sway and leaves the believer free to obey the law of God of which he so heartily approves (7:22).

Just as the law of life in the plant counteracts the downward pull of gravitation, allowing it to express itself in flower and fruit, so the irresistible power of the Spirit leaves the believer free to manifest the graces and produce the fruit of the Spirit (Galatians 5:22, 23).

Fleshly Desires and Passions

"Those who live according to the sinful nature have their minds set on what that nature desires" (ROMANS 8:5).

Though neutral in themselves, the natural desires of our human nature have become debased and perverted through our racial heritage and our own indulgence. One need only read the newspaper to find confirmation of this. "The sinful mind is hostile to God" (v. 7) and manifests itself in unholy ambitions, unholy longings and imaginations, in unkind and censorious speech. Even in our holiest moments the sinful mind intrudes.

But when by a definite act and attitude of commitment we allow the Holy Spirit to control and dominate our minds and personalities (and this is the root meaning of being "filled" with the Spirit), He transforms its tastes and desires. Then it becomes true that "You . . . are controlled not by the sinful nature, but by the Spirit" (v. 9).

It is for us to choose whether we will set our minds on what the sinful nature desires or on what the Spirit desires (v. 8). God cannot do that for us. But the moment we set our weak wills on God's side, the Holy Spirit responds and empowers. Disabilities arising from our sinful natures are not final.

"You, however, are controlled not by the sinful nature but by the Spirit, if the Spirit of God lives in you. And if anyone does not have the Spirit of Christ, he does not belong to Christ" (ROMANS 8:9).

How fickle our hearts are! How easily drawn away from Christ by the lure of the world and the lust of the flesh! But the Holy Spirit is here represented as the permanent caretaker and controller of the heart—monitor, censor, guard, and helper.

Paul draws attention to His almighty power, for He it is who "raised Jesus from the dead." With this mighty Spirit in control of our hearts, at our invitation and with our cooperation, anything is possible. The heart cannot be handicapped or disabled when He is in control.

A Hostile Will

"The sinful mind is hostile to God. It does not submit to God's law, nor can it do so. . . . If you live according to the sinful nature, you will die; but if by the Spirit you put to death the misdeeds of the body, you will live" (ROMANS 8:7, 13).

Most of us are all too familiar with the way in which our wills at times rise up in rebellion against the will of God. When under the impulse of sin the body asserts its desires, the will turns traitor and collaborates with it, and betrays the citadel of Mansoul to the enemy. Here is a grave handicap, but for it there is a divine panacea in the ministry of the Holy Spirit. "If by the Spirit you put to death the misdeeds of the body, you will live." He will enable us to conduct this execution as it is needed, and will also impart the desire and will "to act according to His good purpose (Philippians 2:13).

An Independent Spirit

"Those who are led by the Spirit of God are the sons of God" (ROMANS 8:14).

"I do like to do what I do like to do," said the little daughter of a friend. We all like to run our lives, and in most of us there is an inherent tendency to resent restraint and resist authority imposed from without. Even regeneration does not completely eradicate this desire. The prophet was right when he said, "We all, like sheep, have gone astray, each of us has turned to his own way" (Isaiah 53:6).

The characteristic of the sons of God is that they are led by the Spirit of God. The word *sons* here does not mean "children," but those who share the character, rank, likeness, and privilege of their father—adult sons. Independence of spirit is a mark of spiritual immaturity, or of decadence. Submission to the leading of the Spirit is a sign of mature Christian character; for it is He who imparts "the Spirit of sonship. And by him we cry, 'Abba, Father'" (v. 15). He will gladly lead us when we place the reins of our lives in His hands, and thus deliver us from this handicap.

A Fearful Heart

"You did not receive a spirit that makes you a slave again to fear, but you received the Spirit of sonship" (ROMANS 8:15).

It is not at all difficult to relapse from faith into fear in certain circumstances. All unbidden fear tends to clutch at the heart, and before its onslaught we are impotent. Satan will endeavor to persuade us out of our sonship as he did with Jesus in the desert, with his twice-repeated, "If you are the Son of God." He will attack us on the reality of our conversion, of our call or consecration, and endeavor to shake our confidence in God. It is here that the Holy Spirit unites with our spirit in witness that we are indeed children of God, and called by Him, and that our consecration was real and not counterfeit. Fear and faith are antithetical and incompatible, and the Holy Spirit is the Spirit of faith. When He is in control, the handicap of a fearful heart disappears.

A Prayerless Heart

> "The Spirit helps us in our weakness. We do not know what we ought to pray for, but the Spirit himself intercedes for us with groans that words cannot express" (ROMANS 8:26).

Prayer is so simple that a child can pray, and yet so complex an exercise that the most mature saint would readily subscribe to the apostle's statement. In the face of our natural disinclination to pray, and our weaknesses when we do overcome that disinclination, this assurance of the Spirit's help is doubly welcome.

He will help us in the infirmities of the body—adverse climatic conditions, lack of privacy, difficulty in concentration, physical pain, and discomfort all come within the scope of this divine undertaking. The Spirit of prayer will teach us to pray.

The consistent teaching of this great chapter is that every handicap or disability under which we labor is more than offset by the inworking of the Holy Spirit. But one point needs to be borne in mind: *He can do in us and for us only as much as we trust Him to do.* "According to your faith [trust] it will be done to you" is a spiritual principle of universal application. If we are content to continue in an unsatisfactory prayer-life and do not definitely trust Him to help us in our weakness, we thereby shackle omnipotence. *He will do all we trust Him to do.*

During the Delhi Durbar in India which followed the coronation of King Edward VII of Britain, the Maharajah of Dabah had a plot of land outside Delhi allotted to him. When he went away, he paid a large sum into the local treasury so that the plot of land might be free from the burden of taxes forever. "I, the king, have rested there," he said, "therefore the land shall be free of burdens forever."

Today, those who are near Delhi and have no money may freely claim their place in the spot for which another had paid. They may enjoy without restriction the provision their king had made for them.

So, too, did our King Jesus make "his dwelling among us" (John 1:14) here on earth, and all the blessings of which this chapter speaks have been paid for by Him. We may now enjoy them without restriction, for

> "Therefore, there is now no condemnation [handicap, disability] to those who are in Christ Jesus."

CHAPTER 8

How to Decide Doubtful Matters

"'Everything is permissible'—but not everything
is beneficial. 'Everything is permissible'—
but not everything is constructive"
(1 CORINTHIANS 10:23).

Who of us has not been perplexed at times about the rightness or wrongness of some proposed action? Who has not asked, Is it right to go here or there, to do this or that? These questions are especially troublesome to young people. Can an authoritative and satisfying answer be given to them? Where can it be found?

Many of us older people were brought up under a set of taboos, especially in the area of worldliness. We often yielded to the convictions of others without being fully convinced ourselves. Such "second-hand" attitudes may not lead to a dynamic and healthy spiritual experience. In this very connection Paul said, "Each one should be fully convinced in his own mind" (Romans 14:5).

We must by diligent study of the Scriptures arrive at our own convictions and not indiscriminately adopt those of others. But having said that, we should guard against the idea that there is no place for taboos and prohibitions in the Christian walk. They are found plentifully in both Old and New Testaments.

The Ten Commandments, for example, are all (except for the law of the Sabbath) reiterated and made more searching in the New Testament.

It is true we are no longer under the law as the means of justification, but we are "under law to Christ" as a new way of life.

Paul is as free with his negatives and prohibitions as with his positive exhortations. "Put off," "abstain," "put on," "lay aside," and similar injunctions are characteristic of his letters.

We should remember that the Bible does not legislate in detail for every matter of conduct that might arise. Instead, it enunciates clear principles of conduct which, correctly applied, cover every possible contingency. If God has not given us clear guidance on these matters, how can we be held responsible for failure to do His will?

It is the genius of New Testament Christianity to lay down clear guiding principles rather than to impose a set of rules and regulations. God delights to deal with His children as adults, rather than as children under a tutor. Since this is the case, when we read the Scriptures we should constantly be asking, "What spiritual principles does this passage contain?"

Absolute sincerity of purpose is essential if we are going to discern God's will, for He undertakes to reveal it only to the one who purposes to do it, one who accepts the dictum of Scripture as final.

To approach a doubtful matter with questions such as these—"What's the harm in it?" or, "Everyone's doing it, why not I?" indicates that the matter has already been prejudged and that it is not so much guidance that is wanted as sanction. The mind is almost made up already. The seeker who genuinely desires to find and do God's will as soon as He reveals it will not remain long in doubt.

Eliminating Questions

Here are questions posed in Scripture in another form. To answer them honestly will provide the answer to many borderline problems. Here are the tests.

Will it bring glory to God?

We are exhorted, "Whatever you do, do it all for the glory of God" (1 Corinthians 10:31). If, as the Catechism says, the chief end of man is to glorify God and to enjoy Him forever, then this should be our greatest concern. It should also be *the first test* of any proposed course of action. If the action terminates on self and not on the glory of God, then it should be abandoned.

Is it beneficial?

"'Everything is permissible'—but not everything is beneficial" (1 Corinthians 10:23).

Will it help me to be more effective in my Christian walk, witness, and service?

Is it constructive?

"'Everything is permissible'—but not everything is constructive" (1 Corinthians 10:23).

Is it for the good of others and myself? Is it calculated to build Christians up and to help them to build others up?

Does it tend to enslave?

"'Everything is permissible for me'—but I will not be mastered by anything" (1 Corinthians 6:12).

Even things that are legitimate can become our master. They can so demand our time and attention that we neglect other things of greater importance. For example, excessive secular reading can so enslave the mind of the reader that it vitiates the appetite for reading Scripture and spiritual literature. Such a possibility must be guarded against by strict self-discipline, both as to the quality and quantity of our secular reading.

Will it strengthen me against temptation?

It is of little avail to pray, "Lead us not into temptation," if we voluntarily go where we know we will be exposed to temptation. It is one thing for a uniformed Salvationist to enter a tavern to sell his Gospel magazine, but quite another for a young Christian to go to the same tavern to "celebrate" with his friends. Any place or practice that tends to make sin seem less sinful is to be shunned.

Is it characteristic of the world or of the Father?

"Everything in the world—the cravings of sinful man, the lust of his eyes and the boasting of what he has and does—comes not from the Father but from the world. . . . Do not love the world" (1 JOHN 2:16, 15).

If the proposed action is more characteristic of the world, our course is clear, for "if anyone loves the world, the love of the Father is not in him."

Many relationships, pleasures, and activities—which, while not sins—could be termed "weight" (Hebrews 12:1, KJV), for they impede our progress in the heavenly race, and should therefore be laid aside. G. Campbell Morgan points out that the things that hinder are not all necessarily low or vulgar. They may be in themselves noble things, intellectual things, beautiful things. But if our participation in them clouds the vision of the ultimate goal in the purpose of God and hinders our running, they become weights and hindrances.

Guiding Principles

Let us now consider some principles bearing on doubtful or questionable conduct, which Paul enumerates under the inspiration of the Holy Spirit. In these passages he was dealing with current problems faced by the Roman Christians, which are not dissimilar in essence to those we face today.

Each important spiritual truth and doctrine is treated at length in at least one passage of Scripture. The subject of doubtful things and borderline cases is treated fully in Romans 14, where Paul lays down the following principles:

Liberty of judgment

"One man's faith allows him to eat everything, but another man, whose faith is weak, eats only vegetables. The man who eats everything must not look down on him who does not, and the man who does not eat everything must not condemn the man who does, for God has accepted him" (ROMANS 14:2–3).

The point at issue was whether or not it was permissible to eat meat offered to idols. Well-taught believers, realizing that an idol was nothing at all, felt quite free to eat such meat. But to someone less instructed, it was a cause of stumbling, so they never ate meat. Here was a potential cause of friction where no vital doctrine was involved, so Paul advocates an attitude of tolerance. Within the Christian church there is to be room for genuine difference of opinion. We are to recognize and maintain the rights of our brother to hold opinions opposed to our own.

Right of personal conviction

"One man considers one day more sacred than another; another man considers every day alike. Each one should be fully convinced in his own mind" (ROMANS 14:5).

It is very easy for us, chameleon-like, to take our theological color from the people among whom we are likely to move. The result is that we are as likely to be swayed by mere theological prejudice as by the Word of God.

Paul's exhortation is that we should be fully persuaded in our own minds concerning the matter under review, and not be unduly influenced by someone else, however admirable his or her character and qualifications. We must make our own decisions, for we alone are responsible for our actions, and we have to live with the results.

Accountability to God alone

"Who are you to judge someone else's servant? To his own master he stands or falls" (ROMANS 14:4).

It is God alone to whom we are primarily responsible, for "each one of us will give an account of himself to God" (Romans 14:12). While bearing in mind that we are members of a society in which we have responsibility, Paul emphasizes our *final* accountability to God alone.

Since One is our Master, Christ, anyone else who claims sovereignty over our actions is infringing the "crown rights of the Redeemer." Our appearance at the judgment seat of Christ should deeply influence the actions of all who sincerely wish to do the will of God.

Absence of censoriousness when others differ

"You, then, why do you judge your brother? . . . Let us stop passing judgment on one another" (ROMANS 14:10, 13).

It is not our prerogative to judge and criticize our brother's or sister's actions. That is the right of God alone. Further, we shall all be judged one day, not by one another, but by Christ, so we must be careful. "Make up your mind not to put a stumbling block or obstacle in your brother's way" (Romans 14:13). We are to attribute to him the same degree of sincerity as we would wish him to attribute to us.

Abstinence in the interests of others

"Love does no harm to its neighbor" (ROMANS 13:10).

"It is better not to eat meat or drink wine, or to do anything else that will cause your brother to fall" (ROMANS 14:21).

"We put up with anything rather than hinder the gospel of Christ" (1 CORINTHIANS 9:12).

The disciple is not to live for his own pleasure and profit alone, but is ever to bear in mind the effect his conduct may have on his weaker brother. The freedom of many a moderate drinker has proved the undoing of a weaker man who did not have the same measure of control of his appetite.

We must watch lest our liberty prove a stumbling stone to our brother. It is for us, for Christ's sake, to voluntarily forego our legitimate enjoyment for the sake of our weaker brother. "We who are strong ought to bear with the failings of the weak, and not to please ourselves" (Romans 15:1).

Abstinence from doubtful things

"The man who has doubts is condemned if he eats, because his eating is not from faith, and everything that does not come from faith is sin" (Romans 14:23).

The very fact that we have doubts raises the presumption that the action is questionable. Any action we take should carry with it the positive assurance of faith. The presence of doubt is a call to defer further action until, by prayer and diligent searching of the Scriptures, we arrive at a conviction of the right course.

In this, as in all else, we never lose if we give God the benefit of any doubt. It may be, however, that we have a "weak" conscience on the matter, and it needs to be educated by the Word of God. It is quite possible through tradition or prejudice to have doubts about what the Bible does not condemn.

In this exercise we must not overlook the gracious ministry of the Holy Spirit, whose work it is to "guide [us] into all truth" (John 16:13). "The leadership and discipline of the Holy Spirit through the moral standards of the Word of God—this is the basis of moral living" (source unknown).

CHAPTER 9

Christian Service— Home or Overseas?

"The Lord said to me, 'Go; I will send you far away to the Gentiles'" (ACTS 22:21).

Few crises are so crucial as the ones that determine the whole future course of life. Probably the most important question a young Christian has to answer is: "What is God's will for my life?" On the answer depends the whole trend of the future. Our lives are our own to spend, but we can spend them only once. How important that we spend them wisely!

To think through one's vocation in life is a most important exercise. Everyone with a spark of ambition wants his life to be significant, to count for God and men. A preliminary question that should be settled is whether it should be invested in work in the homeland or in the mission-field. There are so many conflicting voices on this subject that it is not easy to reach a decision. But it is certainly possible to know the will of God on that matter, if we are willing for either. Let us consider some factors that will throw light on the question, "Should my sphere of Christian service be at home or abroad?"

God gave Paul a clear indication of His long-term plan for his life shortly after his conversion: "The Lord said to me, 'Go; I will send you far away to the Gentiles'" (Acts 22:21). This meant that the place of Paul's service would be on foreign soil, and the sphere of his service would not be among his own people, but among Gentiles. As he took steps of faith and obedience, fresh light was given.

We must be firmly convinced that God does and will guide the sincere seeker after His will. We have His assurance: "I will instruct you and teach you in the way you should go; I will counsel you and watch over you" (Psalm 32:8). With such an undertaking from God beneath our feet, we can confidently expect Him to unfold His plan as we sincerely purpose to follow it.

Attitude of heart has an important bearing on the reception of guidance. If the object of our inquiry is to find out the will of God so that we can decide whether or not to do it, we may as well abandon our search at once. God does not respond to such an attitude. But to the person who prays, "Lord, reveal your will to me and I will do it," there will be a certain answer.

It is often said, "I don't feel called to missionary work," as though that disposed of the question. But does one feel a call? Or does one hear a call? More is involved than mere semantics. Did Samuel feel or did he hear God's call when he responded, "Speak, for your servant is listening" (1 Samuel 3:10)? Isaiah said, "I heard the voice of the Lord saying, 'Whom shall I send? And who will go for us?'" (Isaiah 6:8). Did Paul feel or hear the man of Macedonia say, "Come over to Macedonia and help us" (Acts 16:9)? The call of God is not primarily to the emotions.

When we hear the sovereign Lord's call, "All authority in heaven and on earth has been given to me. Therefore go and make disciples of all nations," surely our response is a matter of obedience, not feeling. The command remains, no matter how we feel about it.

To hear the general call of God to all His disciples to engage in worldwide witness is the first element in a call to service. We need no call other than the Scriptures that constitute Christ's Great Commission (Matthew 28:18–20; Luke 24:45–49) to lead us to recognize the general obligation resting on all believers to engage in witness somewhere in the world.

If we see a man drowning and we ourselves can swim, we do not need a special directive to go to his rescue. An inescapable humane obligation rests on us.

There are two ways of facing a potential call to service. We may ask such questions as: "Where will I find self-fulfillment? Where will my gifts and training find fullest utilization? Where will I feel comfortable in my service?" These are valid questions, but are they central?

They were not the questions Paul asked. Once he had his answer to the question, "Who are you, Lord?" (Acts 22:8–10) and knew that Jesus was the Son of God, his next question was, "What shall I do, Lord?" Obediently he rose and went into Damascus. God had already given His message to Ananias, and he passed it on to Paul: "I will show him how much he must suffer for my name" (Acts 9:16). Paul went forward in glad obedience without any question. The Master had spoken.

The other way to approach the question is to ask, "What sphere of service has the Lord prepared for me?" When James and John endeavored to preempt the most prestigious places in Christ's coming kingdom, He checked them with the words, "To sit at my right or left is not for me to grant. These places belong to those for whom they have been prepared" (Mark 10:40). Elsewhere Jesus said, "You did not choose me, but I chose you and appointed you to go and bear fruit" (John 15:16). The right of appointment to a sphere of service does not rest with us but with God.

Note the difference in the two approaches. The first centered on consulting one's own feelings and interests. The other approach was to choose the Lord's sovereign will, recognizing that He is Lord of the harvest.

When the latter course is adopted, the seeker need have no concern about self-fulfillment or the full exploitation of gifts and skills. God's will is "good, and acceptable, and perfect" (Romans 12:2, KJV). He wastes nothing of value.

At Home or Abroad

Can the Great Commission not be fulfilled in the homeland as well as overseas? Is a special call necessary for cross-cultural service overseas? Does the need constitute the call? What are the relative needs and claims at home and abroad? These and other questions clamor to be answered.

There can be no question that a general obligation rests on each Christian to have a part in the spread of the Gospel throughout the world. In His commission Jesus made it clear that there were to be

No geographical limitations—"into all the world."

No racial discrimination—"to all nations."

No class distinctions—"to every creature."

His command can be fulfilled equally at home or abroad. No one form of service is higher or more prestigious than the other, nor is it more pleasing to God. The point at issue is, "Where does He want me to serve?"

What Constitutes a Call?

One good definition of a call is: "A conviction that steadily deepens when faced with the facts of the case, so that sooner or later it becomes a matter of obedience or disobedience."

A call does not come by any stereotyped method; it will vary with the individual. For this reason, while we can profit from the experience of others, we should not expect God to guide us exactly as He guided them.

For example, Philip was directed to work in Samaria as a result of severe persecution. He was later led to the desert by an angel. Then he was directed by the Holy Spirit to join the Ethiopian treasurer in his chariot.

Paul was restrained by the Spirit from entering one field, and constrained by the same Spirit to enter another. He experienced an inward "stop" in his spirit, and later an equally clear "release." The final step that led to his mission to Rome was apparently not the result of any special revelation, but a combination of the exercise of his spiritual judgment and the inner witness of the Spirit. God's method is variety, not uniformity.

God reveals His will to us through His Spirit, and very frequently through His Word. Jesus said that the sheep know their shepherd's voice. When God speaks, we will know that it is He who is speaking.

Dr. K. D. Moynagh testified: "I have found that the voice of God has not been heard in the thunder—not in some sensational call from heaven; nor in the earthquake, some extraordinary experience of upheaval in the circumstances of my life. It has been in a still, small voice—a voice of quiet stillness. God beckons us to come near to Him, and then He speaks by the quiet inner stillness of His peace. He is the umpire in our decisions. Faith accepts quiet guidance, only unbelief demands a miracle."

God can and sometimes does use a vision or dream as one factor in the indication of His will. But dreams and visions do not exempt us from the use of our judgment. It is worthy of note that even in New Testament times a dream was repeated in various forms before it was accepted as guidance (Acts 11:5–10).

The Macedonian Vision

In the case of Paul's vision of the man of Macedonia, it should be remembered that this did not come to him as an initial call. He was already an experienced missionary and had embarked on his second term of service. The vision constituted only one element in his guidance, and it was carefully safeguarded.

When the call came, he had already responded to the general obligation to take the Gospel to the unreached and was seeking the exact place of service God had prepared. When he experienced the restraint in his spirit, he immediately abandoned his own plans. God's set time for Mysia and Bithynia had not yet come—they would hear the good news later. He then stopped at Troas to wait for God to reveal the next step, and it was there he saw the vision (Acts 16:9).

He consulted with his companions, to check his own judgment on the matter. Then, having weighed the factors involved, he made his decision and acted. "We got ready at once to leave for Macedonia, concluding that God had called us to preach the gospel to them" (Acts 16:10). The leading of the vision was therefore in line with the will of God and was witnessed to by the Holy Spirit. There was now no restraint on his spirit, and he had the confirmation of his colleagues. Having arrived at this conviction, even a hostile reception and a lacerated back did not shake this assurance or stifle the songs at midnight.

Relative Claims

Since our Lord's commission can be carried out either at home or abroad, what are the relative needs and claims of these two spheres? Certain potentially eliminating factors may give guidance.

Consistently poor health, nervous disorders, the need of a restricted diet, a tendency toward severe headaches or migraine, or hereditary mental trouble would be indications that probably the sphere of service should be in the homeland. But now that our populations are so polyglot, there is no reason why missionary work cannot be done among ethnic groups at home. However, it would be wise to get a competent doctor's medical opinion of fitness for overseas service.

Certain temperamental conditions would tend to disqualify for service overseas. Anyone who is hypersensitive or of a very high-strung nature would not be a good candidate. Those with a tendency to melancholy or deep depression, who are not able to get on well with others, or who must manage other people would probably not wear well on the mission field.

Spiritual unfruitfulness in the present sphere of service would be a disqualifying factor. There is little point in going overseas to continue to be ineffective. The mere fact of going overseas will make no automatic change in a person, for the change is geographical, not necessarily spiritual. The potential candidate should earnestly seek God's face and comply with His conditions of fruitfulness here before contemplating service overseas (John 12:24).

On the positive side, it is helpful to seek the views of those who have faced the same problems and have seen God open the door.

Ion Keith-Falconer, missionary to Arabia, expressed his conviction in these stirring words:

> While vast continents still lie shrouded in almost utter darkness, and hundreds of millions suffer the

horrors of heathenism and Islam, the burden of proof rests on you to show that the circumstances in which God has placed you were meant to keep you out of the foreign mission field.

In more recent times Bishop Stephen Neill, one of the great missionaries and missiologists of the twentieth century, said:

> I place on record my conviction that the needs of the mission field are always far greater than the needs of the church at home; that no human qualifications, however high, render a man or woman more than adequate for missionary work; that there is no other career which affords such scope for enterprise and creative work; and that in comparison with the slight sacrifice demanded, the reward is great, beyond all measure.

There seems to be no scriptural reason for expecting a clearer call to service overseas than at home, since the difference is only in geography. We need no special call to spread the Gospel; rather we should expect a special call to exempt us from it. A call to overseas service is not essentially different from a call to serve elsewhere.

But is this general obligation sufficient to warrant our engaging in foreign service without a specific call?

Paul had such a call. "The Lord said to Ananias, 'Go! This man is my chosen instrument to carry my name before the Gentiles'" (Acts 9:15). And later Paul testified, "The Lord said to me, 'Go; I will send you far away to the Gentiles'" (Acts 22:21).

Hudson Taylor maintained that a missionary who is not clear on this point will at times be at the mercy of the great enemy. When difficulties arise, when in danger or sickness, he will be tempted to raise the question that should have been settled before he left his native land.

It has been said that facts are the finger of God. If so, it would seem to be a reasonable presumption that if a community is adequately served with the Gospel, the claims of that area should be secondary to those of the inadequately served area. This was one of the lessons Jesus taught in the parable of the one lost sheep and the ninety-nine safe in the fold.

It is undeniable that the homelands are more adequately served than the great blocs of the unevangelized. In most western lands there are churches, Bibles, thousands of Christians, Christian literature, radio and television Gospel broadcasts. But in many areas a seeking soul could not hear the Gospel if they would. These indisputable facts, pondered over, might be the finger of God to the reader.

Paul made two pertinent statements to which we should give heed: "My constant ambition has been to preach the gospel where the name of Christ was previously unknown" (Romans 15:20, J. B. PHILLIPS) and, "I feel myself under a sort of universal obligation. I owe something to all men, from cultured Greek to ignorant savage" (Romans 1:14, J. B. PHILLIPS). Someone said: "I have only one candle to burn. I would rather burn it where people are in darkness than in a land flooded with light."

If you are seeking guidance about missions, become literate in that area. Glean all the information you can. God cannot guide you unless you do your part. Initial guidance may come to you in your quiet time, in a meeting, through a book, through a conversation, or through some Scripture passage interpreted in its context. But do not base your guidance on a single verse. Remember, God guides by His Spirit as well as through the Word, but the Spirit will never lead contrary to the Word.

How Can I Discern God's Will?

- Be unconditionally willing to do it. Your will may need to be redirected.
- Be obedient to light God has already given. If you are not obeying that, why expect more?
- The way ahead may not be revealed all at once—God will show you the next step. "One step is enough for me."
- Seek advice from your pastor or a mature Christian, but don't let anyone else make the decision for you. You will have to live with the issues of that decision. It is your life.
- As you weigh the pros and cons, claim the wisdom promised in James 1:5. Ask the Holy Spirit to sway your mind in the direction of the will of God.
- There is an intellectual component in this exercise. John Wesley said, "God generally guides me by presenting reasons to my mind for acting in a certain way" (not feelings to my heart).
- Make the best decision you can in the light of the facts, believing God has answered your prayer for wisdom. Expect the witness of the Spirit and a growing assurance. Circumstances may confirm your guidance.
- Extraordinary guidance will be the exception rather than the rule, especially as you mature spiritually.
- Be prepared for Satan to challenge your sense of call. He did so with the Master.
- Don't dig up in unbelief what you have sown in faith.

Many Christians have legitimate reasons for not engaging in overseas service and should remain at home without any sense of guilt. But very many young people *could* do so if they *would*. It is a healthy exercise to ask the question, "Why should someone else go and not I?"

CHAPTER 10

There Is a Way Back

*"Take words with you and return to the Lord. Say to
him, 'Forgive all our sins and receive us graciously.'...
I will heal their waywardness and love them freely, for
my anger has turned away from them" (HOSEA 14:2, 4).*

Some of the shortest chapters of the Bible are the weightiest,
the best known, the most cherished of all. Except for
Christ's great parable in Luke 15, Hosea 14 may be the chapter
that is most admirably framed and fitted to meet the case of one
who has turned away from God and is beginning to yearn for
restoration to God's favor.

Derek Kidner happily entitled his exposition of the book of
Hosea *Love to the Loveless,* for that is the moving theme of the
book.

It is all too easy to lose vital touch with God in the sordid
world in which we are called to live and serve. Loss of spiritual
adjustment is not usually deliberate and planned, but it is
nonetheless tragic if the condition is not recognized and dealt
with. The writer to the Hebrews had such a possibility in mind
when he wrote, "May the God of peace ... equip you with
everything good for doing his will" (Hebrews 13:20, 21).

The word he uses for "equip," or "make you perfect" (KJV),
could be used of the repairing of broken bones, or bones that are
out of joint. Its fundamental meaning is "repairing what is

broken." So we could read it as, "put you into correct adjust-ment." A dislocated arm would be an illustration. Its urgent need is to be put back into adjustment with the rest of the body. Only then will the vital force of the body empower the arm for its true function. Likewise, only Christians who are in correct "spiritual adjustment" can fulfill their function in the body of Christ.

The message of Hosea, tenderest of all the prophecies, had this end in view for the alienated nation of Israel. It sprang from the depths of the prophet's own domestic tragedy; hence its pathos. The passages with which we are concerned refer pri-marily to Ephraim, the dominant tribe, and the name is used here of the northern kingdom. The book is a diagnosis of the cause of their spiritual decline, and reveals the way back. It has a contemporary message for the church of today.

The Peril of Partial Consecration

> "What can I do with you, Ephraim?... Your love is like the morning mist, like the early dew that disap-pears" (HOSEA 6:4).

Our age is characterized by superficiality, induced in no small measure by the fleeting images of television. And this superficiality has spilled over into our attitude and reactions to God's message. We seldom give God time to deal with us radi-cally and deeply. Even when we are convicted of failure and sin, we do not usually allow the Holy Spirit to work in us so strong-ly that we come to hate the sin. We lightly assent to the fact that "we are miserable sinners," without seriously and permanently facing it. We act as though a new resolve would take the place of real repentance and renunciation.

God's complaint was that Ephraim's goodness was volatile, vanishing like the morning mist and the early dew. It is not that we do not want the best and highest, or that we do not resolve to do better, but like Ephraim, our resolves are evanescent.

It would seem that Ephraim's fickleness puzzled even God, causing Him to exclaim, "What can I do with you, Ephraim?" Our superficiality and fickleness, too, must perplex God after all He has done for us. But for our encouragement we can remember that under the influence of the Holy Spirit, Simon the volatile was changed into Peter the rock.

The Peril of Partial Sanctification

"Ephraim is a flat cake not turned over" (HOSEA 7:8).

This pictorial figure was familiar to the Israelite. Most cooks have experienced the chagrin of finding their cake cooked on the outside but doughy inside. The cake referred to here was flat and cooked on a griddle; and not having been turned over, it was burnt on one side and raw on the other.

Many of us are like this in character—overdeveloped in some aspects, but deficient in others. Progress has been excellent in some areas, but retarded in others. All of us are to some extent only partially sanctified, because we have not turned some parts of our lives toward the purifying fire of the Holy Spirit.

Some are strong in Bible knowledge but weak in graciousness. Others are strong in orthodoxy but weak in Christian love. Still others are generous in giving but violent in temper. One-sided development is true of us all. Jesus alone was completely sanctified and symmetrical in character—"full of grace and truth." In Him we see in perfect balance "the goodness and severity of God" (Romans 11:22, KJV). It could never be said of Him that He was a cake not turned.

It is a common temptation to overdo some forms of work we enjoy but to neglect hidden or less congenial tasks. We tend to cultivate our strong points while neglecting the weak ones. The scholar avidly feeds his mind but tends to neglect his body, while with athletes it is often the reverse. Scripture enjoins cultivation of the weak points of our characters so that we may "stand firm in all the will of God, mature and fully assured" (Colossians 4:12).

The reassuring fact is that the fire under the cake is still burning. There is yet time for the cake to be turned and the baking process completed. It is for us to turn the imperfect and unfinished facets of our characters toward the fire of the Holy Spirit.

The Peril of Incomplete Separation

"Ephraim is joined to idols. Leave him alone" (HOSEA 4:17).

"Ephraim mixes with the nations" (HOSEA 7:8).

Christians are to be a separated people. But some evangelical circles advocate a type of separation that so puts us out of touch with worldly people that we are unable to reach them for Christ. When Jesus said to His disciples, "You are the salt of the earth" (Matthew 5:13), He did not envisage the salt being on one plate and the meat on another. As someone said, the place for the salt is in the soup, not the shaker.

Jesus never suggested that Christians should isolate themselves from worldly people and leave them for the devil. He Himself was the object of bitter criticism by the Pharisees because He refused to practice this form of separation. "This man welcomes sinners and eats with them," they sneered.

One form of separation, however, is not only right but obligatory. Ephraim must separate himself from idols and from allegiance with the ungodly nations who worshiped them.

The statement concerning Ephraim and his idols is frequently misread, as though God were saying, "Well, if Ephraim will have his idols, let him have them. I am through with him."

But that is exactly what God is not saying. His lament was, "How can I give you up, Ephraim?" (Hosea 11:8). It was not that God was going to abandon Ephraim, but He was warning the kingdom of Judah not to follow his bad example. "If he will go after his idols, don't you follow him." *Leave him alone* is the divine warning to Judah.

There are many worldly associations that must be broken, but it is to be the separation of *insulation* rather than *isolation*. Or even better, the separation of the bride to the bridegroom. Jesus was "holy, blameless, pure, set apart from sinners" (Hebrews 7:26), but His separation was moral and spiritual, not physical. In this He left us an example to follow.

The Peril of Unconscious Deterioration

"Foreigners sap his strength, *but he does not realize it.*
His hair is sprinkled with gray, but he does not notice"
(HOSEA 7:9, emphasis added).

Gray hairs are an unwelcome sign of waning virility. They come unfelt and unannounced. Few go gray in a night. Even so, spiritual decline is not necessarily conscious or sudden. Backsliding is not usually determined and deliberate. Spiritual vision and enthusiasm always tend to wane if not carefully nurtured.

The flesh is weak, and we are subject to the hostile attention of our adversary.

Ephraim's unconscious deterioration began with an unholy alliance with idolatrous Assyria, who led them into that sinful worship. Idolatry and immorality usually run together in double harness, with a consequent weakening of the whole fabric of the nation. Ephraim is counseled to say:

> "Assyria cannot save us; we will not mount war-horses.
> We will never again say, 'Our gods' to what our own hands have made" (HOSEA 14:3).

The warning is equally applicable to us, and we should be at pains to discover whether gray hairs, premature signs of spiritual senility, are appearing in our private lives. It is possible to keep up outward appearances of godliness when spiritual atrophy is far advanced.

Ignorance of our true state may be the result of having neglected to look searchingly at our life in the mirror of the Word of God. This mirror would reveal to us—if we cared to see it—the gray hairs, the startling difference between the actual and the ideal. Spiritual decline often begins when we are too busy (even in Christian work) to periodically measure ourselves by the divine standard and take remedial action.

The tragedy of Ephraim's condition is revealed in two clauses: "He does not realize it," and "He does not notice." Unconscious deterioration! The only satisfactory and permanent way to dispose of gray hairs is not to dye them (as we sometimes do), but to pull them out by the roots. The Corinthian believers were counseled to do this: "Let us purify ourselves from everything that contaminates body and spirit" (2 Corinthians 7:1).

This involves a decisive act of the will. There is a cleansing, a plucking out, which God will not do for us. Our part is to purpose to have done with our sin, whatever it may be, and the Lord responds, "I will cleanse you from all your impurities and from all your idols" (Ezekiel 36:25).

The Way Back

We should thank God that He does not stop with a diagnosis of the malady, but graciously prescribes and provides the cure.

> "Return, O Israel, to the LORD your God... Take words with you... Say to him, 'Forgive all our sins, and receive us graciously'" (HOSEA 14:1,2).

God first enjoins *repentance*. Not a vague and general confession, but a specific and personal outpouring of a contrite heart. Our sins have been committed individually, and we should name them before Him and seek forgiveness.

> *Repentance is to leave*
> *The sins we loved before,*
> *And show that we in earnest grieve*
> *By doing them no more.*

Then there is to be *renunciation of entangling alliances*. Association with the ruthless Assyrians and reliance on the forbidden Egyptian horses had been Ephraim's undoing, and such alliances must be terminated. They must say, "Assyria cannot save us, we will not mount war-horses." All idols must be renounced. "We will never again say, 'Our gods' to what our own hands have made" (14:3). God will tolerate nothing that takes the place which is His by right.

What a welcome is promised to Ephraim when he fulfills these terms and returns to the Lord! "I will heal their waywardness and love them freely, for my anger has turned away from them" (Hosea 14:4).

Did Ephraim's love for God disappear like the morning mist? Then hear God's gracious assurance: "I have swept away your offenses like a cloud, your sins like the morning mist. Return to me, for I have redeemed you" (Isaiah 44:22).

Bonus Blessings

As though these blessings were not enough for a penitent and restored Ephraim, three more are promised.

Freshness

"I will be like the dew to Israel" (Hosea 14:5). Ephraim's volatile goodness, which vanished like the morning dew, is replaced by the refreshing dew of God. In the East, dew is the main source of renewal of plant life. Without it vegetation would die. It is not a luxury but a necessity. The readjusted life that had previously been dry and barren is now dew-drenched and fresh. The renewing of the Holy Spirit makes all things new. Dew received and enjoyed will become dew imparted. "The remnant of Jacob will be in the midst of many peoples, like dew from the LORD" (Micah 5:7). Our lives can be not only perennially refreshed, but can continually refresh others.

Fragrance

The freshness of the dew released the fragrance of the flower. God said, "I will be like the dew to Israel; he will blossom like a lily . . . his fragrance like a cedar of Lebanon" (Hosea 14:5, 6).

What is so delicate and subtle a thing as a fragrance? Its presence cannot be mistaken. It penetrates closed doors and fills the house. Through spending time in the presence of the Lord, the apostles came away with His unmistakable fragrance about them, and the hostile authorities "took note that these men had been with Jesus" (Acts 4:13).

Fruitfulness

But freshness and fragrance, delightful though they are, are not an end in themselves. Fruitfulness is the end and goal of all nature. Hosea tells us that the same Lord who sends the dew and produces the fragrance is also the source of fruitfulness. "O Ephraim, I am like a green pine tree; *your fruitfulness comes from me*" (emphasis added).

A broken branch, out of adjustment with the tree, produces no fruit to perfection. A believer who is out of touch, out of adjustment with God, does not produce the fruit of the Spirit. But once he or she returns to the Lord, fruitfulness in character and service becomes a reality.

CHAPTER 11

The Paradox of Sanctification

*"Continue to work out your salvation with fear
and trembling, for it is God who works in you
to will and to act according to his good purpose"
(PHILIPPIANS 2:12, 13).*

"Let go and let God" is a motto that has been around for many years. It sounds pious, and with qualifications is a valid exhortation, but without those qualifications it is a dangerous half-truth, for it can induce a harmful passivity.

True, we must "let go" every sin and hindering encumbrance. But we must not let go in the sense of adopting a passive attitude toward what God says is our responsibility. It is also true that we must "let God" do what He has promised, and what He alone can do. But we must not "let God," in the sense of expecting Him to do what He says is our responsibility. The Christian life calls for positive moral action and obedience on our part, as well as a confident expectation that God will do all He has promised.

One of Paul's favorite methods of presenting spiritual truth was by making use of paradox, which has been defined as "an apparent contradiction, a contradiction in terms—but not in its deep reality. Whenever in Scripture we find language apparently self-contradictory, or in apparent conflict with what is elsewhere said, we may depend on it there is some great harmony deep down below the surface, yearning for expression" (H. C. Mabie).

For example, Paul asserts that we have died and yet we live. He claimed to be sorrowful yet always rejoicing. Having nothing, he yet possessed all things. He was poor, yet made many rich. The passage we are considering is another example: "Work out your salvation . . . for it is God who works in you."

There are two complementary aspects of holy living—what God does, and what we must do. All idea of passively waiting for God to perform the miracle of deliverance and sanctification without our active cooperation is excluded. There must be the cooperation of the human with the divine, and it is fatal to ignore or play down either aspect.

Admittedly it is difficult sometimes to determine where God's part ends and man's begins, but it is the ministry of the Holy Spirit to illumine the minds of those who are honestly seeking to know God's truth on this point.

While faith is a vital element in sanctification, it is not attained apart from man's cooperation. He is exhorted to "put off" his old self, and to "put on" the new self (Ephesians 4:22, 24). While he is to reckon that "those who belong to Christ Jesus have crucified the sinful nature with its passions and desires" (Galatians 5:24), he is also exhorted, "By the Spirit . . . put to death the misdeeds of the body" (Romans 8:13).

The perplexity increases when we endeavor to reconcile our text with Paul's statement that "to the man who does not work, but trusts God who justifies the wicked, his faith is credited as righteousness" (Romans 4:5).

The answer is that the two ideas are complementary, not contradictory, as we shall see.

The Exhortation to Work

"Continue to work out your salvation with fear and trembling."

The strength of theological bias is evidenced in Monsignor Ronald Knox's translation of this passage: "You must work to earn your salvation in anxious fear." But the verse neither says nor means that. Paul explicitly said that the Philippian Christians were to work out "your [own] salvation," a salvation that was already their possession, not one which they were to earn by feverish and fear-ridden endeavor. There is a world of difference between "work out" and "work for."

Paul is saying in effect, "You have been given an estate; now go to work and develop its hidden resources." *Salvation* is a spacious word, and in Scripture it is used of the believing person in three senses:

He *has been saved* from sin's guilt and penalty.
He *will yet be saved* from sin's defiling presence.
He *is now being saved* from its power.

So the past justification, the present sanctification, and the future glorification are all involved in the expression "your salvation."

The expression "work out" carries the idea of working out to an ultimate goal, as in a scientific or mathematical problem. The question of the believer's salvation or standing before God is not in view in the passage, nor is there room for the idea that our sanctification is something completed in a high moment of surrender to Christ. It is true that full surrender to Christ is necessary for full sanctification, but the crisis of surrender is only the initiation of the process. We have a life job on our hands.

Paul protested: "Not that I have already obtained all this, or have already been made perfect" (Philippians 3:12).

Sanctification is not automatic or the result of mere efflux-ion of time. The free agency of man in cooperating with God is involved. God sends the sun and rain, provides soil and seed, but there would be no crop if the farmer did not plow and fertilize, sow and reap.

On one occasion George Muller, a man of great faith, was approached by a young man who was experiencing difficulty in defeating the pull of the blankets in order to have a time of personal devotion. He asked Mr. Müller if he would pray that he might be able to get up in the morning. To his surprise, the answer was a firm negative. But the old man went on to say: "Young man, if you will get one leg out of bed tomorrow morning, I will ask the Lord to help you get the other one out."

This was not only common sense, but sound theology. There is a part that only God can play in our full salvation and a part which only man can perform. But as man fulfills the part assigned to him the Holy Spirit forms the transmission line along which the enabling power flows from God. God always responds to faith.

So then we are to work out to a finish, in terms of our own living and character, the glories inherent in our own salvation. But in what spirit are we to do it? "In anxious fear," as Knox suggests? Surely not. This would be contrary to the whole spirit of the gospel. Marven Vincent gives the meaning as, "Not in slavish terror, but wholesome serious caution." It has been suggested that Paul exhorts as though he were an Arminian, but in addressing God, he prays like a Calvinist and seems to feel no inconsistency in doing so.

Paul's exhortation is a warning against the peril of self-confidence in working out our salvation. It is to be done in the spirit of dependence on the Holy Spirit, as he suggests in another connection: "If *by the Spirit* you put to death the misdeeds of the body, you will live" (Romans 8:13, emphasis added).

The Enablement to Work

"It is God who works in you."

God does not exhort us to action without providing adequate motive and incentive to encourage us to attain the highest in life and character. In this clause we find a double motive.

The indwelling of God

We are not left to our own unaided resources, dependent on a mere external stimulus. The eternal triune God dwells in us. Hear what Jesus says on this point:

> "If anyone loves me, he will obey my teaching. My Father will love him *and we will come to him and make our home with him. . . .* The Spirit of truth. . . . *lives with you and will be in* you" (JOHN 14:23, 17, emphasis added).

Jesus' promise is surely a strong incentive to induce believers to cooperate with their indwelling Guest with all His powers.

The inworking of God

Not only does the omnipotent God dwell in the believer's heart, but He is at work there as the active agent in our sanctification, and God's working is effectual.

How impossible it would be for man to force tons of water through solid wood. Yet every day this miracle is performed a thousand times as the sap rises in the tree.

With this consciousness of the divine inworking, Paul exclaimed, "I can do everything through [Christ] who gives me strength" (Philippians 4:13). Note that the word *everything* does not indicate that he could do "all things in the universe," but implied that he could do everything that it was the good pleasure of God for him to do. Within the sphere of God's will, he enjoyed a sort of omnipotence.

The Extent of God's Working

"To will and to act according to his good purpose."

Here is another aspect of the paradox. God works within me to will and to act, yet the willing and acting are mine. But it should be noted that God does not will *instead* of me, or act *instead* of me. In sanctification God and man are joined in indissoluble partnership, and all efforts to separate the respective spheres of activity are abortive. I *will*, but God works the will in me. I *act,* but God supplies the power.

The disposition

The problem posed in Romans 7 is summarized in verse 18: "I have the desire to do what is good, but I cannot carry it out." The pagan Virgil mourned: "I see a better course, and I approve, but I follow the worse." He lacked the disposition to do the better thing, although with his mind he approved it. Even the regenerate person is weak so long as he tries to do the will of God by virtue of his regeneration—he finds too often that at the crucial moment his will is paralyzed.

In his translation of this verse Arthur S. Way presents the activity of God as "supplying the impulse, giving you the power to resolve and the will to perform the execution of His good pleasure." We are not cast back on our own resources. We have the benefits accruing from the death and resurrection of Christ, and His gift of the Holy Spirit through whose activity those benefits become operative in our lives.

But I must do the choosing. God does not impart His power apart from the active participation and cooperation of our wills. Once I put my weak will on God's side, and despite my own volitional weakness choose His will, it becomes possible for the Holy Spirit to empower my vitiated will.

The doing

Even after the right impulse has been supplied by God giving the power to resolve, it still remains for me to act. Sanctification is essentially positive; it does not consist merely in not doing wrong things. In exercise of the power imparted by God's Spirit, I am now able to perform "his good purpose." In myself, I am no stronger; but with the divine indwelling and inworking, I am no longer the plaything of weakness and sin.

> *Lord, Thou canst work in me*
> *The will to do Thy will,*
> *Lord, Thou canst work in me to work,*
> *Thy pleasure to fulfill.*

No more apt illustration of the cooperation of man is recorded than that of the man with the shriveled hand (Matthew 12:9–13). Try as he would, no attempted exercise of his will produced any effect on the paralyzed muscles. When Jesus commanded him to stretch out his hand, a natural reaction would be for him to say, "I have tried to do so a thousand times, but with no effect. Is there any reason to expect anything different the thousand-and-first time?"

But faith had been kindled in his heart, and in response to the Lord's command, he exercised his will. To his surprise and joy the shriveled hand responded, whole as the other. The activity of faith had released the power of God.

As in the physical, so in the spiritual—"Everything is possible for him who believes" (Mark 9:23).

> *'Twas most impossible of all*
> *That here in me sin's reign should cease.*
> *Yet shall it be? I know it shall,*
> *'Tis certain, though impossible.*
> *The thing impossible shall be,*
> *All things are possible to me.*
>
> CHARLES WESLEY

CHAPTER 12

Ambition That God Approves

*"It has always been my ambition to preach
the gospel where Christ was not known, so that
I would not be building on someone
else's foundation" (ROMANS 15:20).*

"Cromwell, I charge thee, fling away ambition: by that sin fell the angels; how can man, then . . . hope to win by it?"

When Shakespeare put these words into the mouth of Cardinal Wolsey, was he echoing the teaching of Scripture, or was it mere worldly wisdom? Is ambition necessarily a base and unworthy quality? Is it indeed "the last infirmity of noble minds" (source unknown)?

Scripture does teach that there is an ambition that warrants these strictures, but it also advocates an ambition that is worthy to be cherished. Ambition that exclusively centers around and terminates on oneself is unworthy. An ambition in which the glory of God is central is not only legitimate, but positively praiseworthy.

A Master Ambition

Many able people fail of worthwhile achievement simply because they have no master ambition that will unify and integrate life's activities. They live haphazardly, and not like the disciplined Paul who said, "One thing I do" (Philippians 3:13).

Their father told this story of the famous Webster brothers, Daniel and Ezekiel. When he found the boys lounging around listlessly, he asked, "What are you doing, Ezekiel?" "Doing nothing," was the reply. "And what are you doing, Daniel?" "Helping Zeke, sir." That is the occupation of too many.

If we are to achieve a worthy ambition, it will require a whole-hearted abandonment to the task, such as the orator Demosthenes demonstrated in the pursuit of oratorical excellence.

In his book *Life Power,* Arthur T. Pierson records that when Demosthenes first appeared on the stage, he was hissed and booed. His voice was harsh and weak, his appearance was not prepossessing, he made ugly grimaces as he spoke, he had a painful stammer and an ugly hitching of his shoulder. However, he determined that his fellow-citizens would yet hang on his words. To this end he gave himself day and night to the study and practice of elocution.

He shaved half of his head so that he would not be tempted into the involvements of social life. To overcome his stammer, he recited his lines with pebbles in his mouth. He matched his orations with the thunders of the Aegean Sea so that his voice might gain in volume. The ugly hitching of his shoulder he corrected by standing under a suspended sword with the point resting on his shoulder. Any facial distortions he corrected by practicing in front of a mirror.

Is it surprising that when his nation was threatened with invasion by Philip, Demosthenes was one of the orators chosen to inspire the nation to action? When the first orator finished a remarkable speech, the crowd said, "What marvelous oratory!" But when Demosthenes reached his peroration, the people cried out with one voice, "Come, let us fight Philip!" His voice was heard by his fellow-citizens.

Unworthy Ambition

Worldly ambition finds expression in three main areas: to build a reputation, to amass wealth, to wield power. The fatal flaw in these ambitions is that they all terminate on self and not God.

Ambition of that sort does not usually ennoble. It engenders envy, jealousy, and strife. It is impatient of the consideration due to others and will go to any lengths to achieve its ends. It is the force that drives the "successful" businessman to crush his weaker or more scrupulous competitor. It will descend to white-collar crime.

But how tawdry and unsubstantial are its rewards! How trivial its achievements when viewed in the light of eternity! The ambition of a Napoleon or a Hitler brought them moments of glory, but also everlasting shame. Such an ambition is the antithesis of the Spirit of the cross of Christ.

It is possible to entertain an unworthy ambition in religious as well as worldly associations. Before their transforming experience on the Day of Pentecost, two of Christ's intimates, James and John, prevailed on their doting mother to use her influence with Jesus to gain preferment for them in Christ's coming kingdom. They stooped to petty intrigue to exclude the other claimants to the posts of supreme privilege and power. Even the Last Supper was not too sacred an occasion to be marred by selfish place-seeking. Nor were the ten apostles free from the same unworthy ambition, else why were they so indignant at James and John for forestalling them (Mark 10:41)? They had yet to master the difficult lesson of humility, and through a very bitter experience.

The ambition God approves is far other. The obedient disciple lives by an entirely different scale of values. God-approved ambition must be pure and noble, tinged with self-abnegation and self-sacrifice. Since he or she belongs to Christ—body, intellect, emotions, and will—any honor or glory that may come to them belongs to their master. Like Him the disciple will cherish an ambition to give rather than to receive, to serve rather than to be served (Mark 10:45). To use their talents for the Master, rather than to debase them by using them for self-aggrandizement or self-indulgence.

The Revealing Motive

The character of an ambition is determined by the underlying motive. Whether it is laudable or base is revealed in the motivation that inspired it. The Lord's message to Baruch through Jeremiah was: "Should you then seek great things *for yourself?* Seek them not" (Jeremiah 45:5, emphasis added).

In His Sermon on the Mount Jesus counseled: "Do not store up *for yourselves* treasures on earth" (Matthew 6:19, emphasis added). The wrong does not lie in the ambition itself, but in the motive that inspired it. "For yourself"—these are the telltale words. An intensely ambitious man himself, Paul encouraged others to aim high in this regard by citing himself as an example.

"I press on toward the goal to win the prize" (PHILIPPIANS 3:14).

"Run in such a way as to get the prize" (1 CORINTHIANS 9:24).

In three of his letters, Paul's other-worldly ambitions appear almost incidentally.

> "We make it our goal [ambition] to please him, whether we are at home in the body or away from it" (2 CORINTHIANS 5:9).

> "Make it your ambition to lead a quiet life, to mind your own business and to work with your hands" (1 THESSALONIANS 4:11).

> "It has always been my ambition to preach the gospel where Christ was not known" (ROMANS 15:20).

All his ambitions centered in Christ.

David Brainerd was missionary to American Indians. So consumed was he with a passion to bring glory to Christ in winning souls for His kingdom that he wrote in his diary, "I cared not where or how I lived, or what hardships I endured, could I but win souls for Christ. While I was asleep I dreamt of such things, and when I waked the first thing I thought of was the winning of souls to Christ."

The supreme ambition of George Whitefield, "the seraphic evangelist," found expression in the single sentence: "If God did not give me souls, I believe I should die."

An Old Testament Illustration

One of the great examples of a holy ambition of which God approved is given in this paragraph:

> "Jabez was more honorable than his brothers. His mother had named him Jabez, saying, 'I gave birth to him in pain.' Jabez cried out to the God of Israel, 'Oh,

that you would bless me and enlarge my territory! Let
your hand be with me, and keep me from harm so that
I will be free from pain.' And God granted his request"
(1 CHRONICLES 4:9–10).

This brief passage affords insight into the character and ambitions of the one man whom God singled out for honorable men-
tion from among his contemporaries. It is a remarkable thumbnail
sketch that discloses the ambition which made Jabez "more honorable than his brothers." Its very setting—a veritable oasis in a wilder-
ness of the dead—would indicate the importance God attached to
this man's attainments. When God troubles to preserve the epitaph
of one man out of millions, and gives it in such concise and pregnant language, it will undoubtedly repay detailed study.

Before passing on to the subject of Jabez's ambition, two lessons from his life are worthy of note.

Obscurity need not shadow a life

Jabez's epitaph contains only the bare essentials relevant to
the divine purpose. No indication is given of his wealth, gifts, or
popularity; only that he became more honorable than his brothers. Of him alone does God preserve a record for posterity.

Church history teaches that God sometimes takes up
obscure men and women and uses them to a unique degree,
while passing by people of far greater gift. Jabez sprang out of
obscurity into age-long prominence because of his prayer life.
His recorded prayer provides the key to his life.

Disabilities need not disqualify in the race of life

Jabez was born with a great temperamental handicap. This
is implicit in the name given to him by his mother—Jabez

means "sorrowful." Tragedy may have struck before his birth and shadowed his entry into the world. Prenatal influence can greatly affect the nature of a child, and apparently this baby did not escape its effects. Indeed, it may be that overcoming this disability is what made him great.

Although his nature apparently was set in a minor key, and he inherited a bias toward pessimism, he soared above his brothers who inherited no such disability.

One missionary friend of mine whose work was greatly blessed, and whose books have blessed tens of thousands, once confided to me, "All my life I have had to battle against depression." And yet those of us who knew her never guessed that she had this tendency. She soared above it and triumphed through Christ.

God is sympathetic toward a holy ambition

Jabez cherished an ambition to which God responded magnificently. His four ambitions were ambitions indeed, and on the surface might appear selfish. But the fact that "God granted his request" indicated that his underlying motive was God's glory rather than self-aggrandizement. God does not honor unworthy motives, nor does He answer self-centered petitions. God delighted to honor Jabez because he delighted to honor God. "Those who honor me I will honor" (1 Samuel 2:30) is an abiding principle.

The fourfold petition of his prayer voiced the deepest aspiration of his heart.

Divine enrichment

"Oh, that you would bless me!" (1 CHRONICLES 4:10).

Jabez qualified for the beatitude, "Blessed are those who hunger and thirst for righteousness." No ordinary blessing would satisfy him. He yearned for something far surpassing his past experience. God's ear is always open to such a plea, for a true spiritual blessing always ennobles character.

"And God granted his request."

Divine enlargement

"Oh, that you would . . . enlarge my territory!"

His primary concern was probably for an increase of territory that would create a larger sphere of influence rather than for personal aggrandizement. It is not necessarily an unworthy ambition to long for a wider sphere of influence.

Some of our hymns breathe pious sentiment, but they are not always sound theology and do not always stand close analysis. Here is one:

Content to fill a little space, if God be glorified.

This is of course a worthy sentiment. We must be willing to glorify God in "a little space" if that is where He puts us. Until we qualify there, it is unlikely that we will be promoted. But the implication of this couplet—probably unintentional—is that God can be glorified more in a little space than in a larger sphere.

Should we not be ambitious to fill a *larger* sphere if we can thereby bring more glory to God and influence more people for Him? He needs great men and women. He does not want all of His children filling only the small spheres of life. He needs those who will serve Him loyally and glorify Him in positions of great responsibility. Such contentment as the hymn advocates could spring from spiritual inertia and unwillingness to pay the price of occupying larger territory for Christ.

Would not William Carey's motto be more worthy of our Master?

Attempt great things for God!
Expect great things from God!
Dare a bolder programme!
Dwell in an ampler world!
Launch out into the deep!

God is looking for men and women who, like Jabez, are discontented with a limited opportunity in a world where such unmet needs abound. Our ambition should be for a wider influence for God, a deeper love for God, a stronger faith in God, and a growing knowledge of God. Provided our motivation is right, God will not deny our petition for divine enlargement.

"And God granted his request."

Divine enablement

"Let your hand be with me."

Enlarged territory involves more responsibility and imposes greater demands. Jabez knew that he would require a power greater than his own to possess and develop a larger territory for God. God's hand represents His mighty power. John the Baptist moved his nation so mightily because "the Lord's hand was with him" (Luke 1:66). So it was with Jabez.

"And God granted his request."

Divine environment

"Keep me from evil, that it may not grieve me!"

Jabez well knew the inevitable peril of enlarged territory—it would invite the hostile attention of his enemies. Attempting great things for God could mean increased activity on the part of Satan. So his prayer is appropriate in all ages. Did not our Lord pray, "My prayer is . . . that you protect them from the evil one" (John 17:15)?

We are always vulnerable to Satan's attacks, and therefore we need to be watchful, and walk in humble dependence on God. In his conscious need Jabez prayed for a sense of God's environing presence.

"And God granted his request."

CHAPTER 13

The Strategic Use of Time

"Make the best use of your time "
(EPHESIANS 5:16, PHILLIPS).

Time is the Christian's most precious commodity, and yet it is often spent thoughtlessly or even recklessly. It seems to be in perennially short supply. The stock excuse offered for neglected duty is: "I didn't have time."

We are sincere when we say it, but it would often be nearer the truth if we confessed, "I haven't used my time to the best advantage," or "I am disorganized; I have got my priorities wrong." The excuse of insufficient time is seldom heard on the lips of the busiest people. Our real problem is not insufficiency of time, but how to use strategically the time that we do have.

Care must be taken in the selection of priorities. Comparative opportunities and responsibilities should be diligently weighed, for we cannot afford to squander time on things of only secondary importance while primary things are screaming for attention. If we are to be our best for God, we must select and reject, and concentrate on the primary.

In what is recognized as one of the world's greatest sermons, Horace Bushnell preached on the theme: *Every life, a plan of God.* In it this illuminating paragraph occurs:

> Every human soul has a complete and perfect plan
> cherished for it in the heart of God, a divine biography

which it enters into life to live. This life, rightly unfolded, will be a complete and beautiful whole, led on by
God and unfolded by His secret nurture, as the trees
and the flowers by the secret nurture of the world.

This paragraph highlights a wonderful truth, which rightly
apprehended could impart a dignity and significance to the
humblest life. It accords with Paul's claim that "we are God's
workmanship, created in Christ Jesus to do good works, which
God prepared in advance for us to do" (Ephesians 2:10).

If it is true, the corollary is that there are enough hours in
each day for us to fulfill God's perfect and particular plan for our
lives.

Christ's Exemplary Use of Time

Our Lord moved through life with majestic and measured
tread, never in haste though always thronged by demanding
crowds. He never gave those who sought His help a sense that
He had any more important concerns than their particular
interests.

What was the secret of His serenity? Knowing that everyone's
life is a plan of God, He recognized that His life and all the conditions in which it was to be worked out were under His Father's
sovereign control. Time therefore had no power over Him.

On several occasions He asserted that His hour had not yet
come. Implicit in this claim was the conviction that His Father's
plan had been drawn with such meticulous care and accuracy
that every hour was accounted for, and was adjusted to the over-
all purpose of His life. His calendar had been arranged, and His
sole concern was to fulfill the assigned work in the allotted
hours (John 7:6; 12:23, 27; 17:1).

Not even His much-loved mother was allowed to interfere with this divinely planned timetable (John 2:4). Deep human affection could not be permitted to alter His schedule by two days, or His Father's plan would be marred (John 11:6–9). Small wonder, then, that at the end of His life He could review it with complacency and utter the self-approving words: "I have brought you glory on earth by completing the work you gave me to do" (John 17:4).

No part of His work had been marred by undue haste, nor had it been imperfectly completed through lack of time. He found sufficient hours in the day to do all the will of God. His corrective word to the disciples, "Are there not twelve hours of daylight?" (John 11:9), seems to suggest His quiet, steady confidence in His Father's purpose, and this imparted courage even in the face of enemies and danger.

Interruptions did not disturb His serenity, because they had already been provided for in His Father's plan. The wrath of His adversaries would have to await His "hour." Even though there would not always be a chance to eat, there would be time for all God intended Him to do (Mark 6:31). Do we share His confidence?

It is easy to stand off and admire these qualities in the Master which are so lacking in our own lives. But He is to be followed, not admired, and He left us an example in this as in all else. "As the Father has sent me," He said, "I am sending you" (John 20:21). He who sends will enable the performance.

What Is Time?

Is it the ticking of a clock? The moving of a shadow? Calendar and clock are only mechanical devices by which we record our consciousness of time, not time itself. As we commonly use the word, it means *duration*, or a stretch of duration during which things happen. Another definition is, "duration turned to account." John R. Mott viewed time as "our lives measured out for work; the measure of the capacity of ourselves."

Paul counseled the Ephesian Christians to buy up the opportunities (Ephesians 5:16), for time is opportunity. It becomes ours by purchase—it has to be bought. We exchange it for certain activities, important or otherwise, and herein lies the value of a planned life. Time is a God-given stewardship for which we must render an account. Our use of it will determine our contribution to our own generation. The difference between one person and another lies largely in his or her use of time.

"All attainments and achievements are conditioned by the full use of time," wrote one of the masters of that art. "If we progress in the economy of time, we are learning to live. If we fail here, we fail everywhere. No man is or does more than his time allows him to do" (source unknown).

In his book *Holy Living,* old Jeremy Taylor wrote: "God hath given man a short time here on earth, yet upon this short time eternity depends. No man is a better master than he that lays out his time upon God."

The solemn thing about time is that it can be lost. And once lost, it cannot be retrieved. It is permanently lost. How important, then, that we make full use of the time allotted to us. The following quotation on a sundial emphasizes this truth:

> *The shadow by my finger cast*
> *Divides the future from the past.*
> *Before it stands the unborn hour*
> *In darkness and beyond thy power.*
> *Behind its unreturning line*

The vanished hour, no longer thine.
One hour alone is in thy hands,
The Now *on which the shadow stands.*

Sometimes we have so much to do that we increase the hours of the days by reducing sleep. This can be a highly dangerous expedient if pressed too far. The truth is that if we do not have sufficient time to discharge our responsibilities, either we have undertaken tasks not laid on us by the Lord, or we are not making strategic use of the time He has given us.

It would be a revealing experiment to keep an hour-by-hour analysis of the way we spend our time for a whole week. Put the clock on yourself, and you will be surprised to find that you have much more time available than you are using constructively.

Each week has 168 hours. Allow a generous 56 hours for rest and sleep; 21 hours for meals; 56 hours for work and study. There still remain 35 hours, or 5 hours a day unaccounted for. What happens to them? How are they invested?

These are the crucial hours that determine whether our lives will be commonplace or extraordinary. These are the hours that we allow to slip from us. Our spare time—and it is not usually true to say we have no spare time—is at once our opportunity or our danger.

Mastery of Time

"I think one of the cant phrases of our day is the familiar one by which we express our permanent want of time," wrote J. H. Jowett. "We repeat it so often that by the very repetition we have deceived ourselves into believing it. It is never the supremely busy who have no time. So compact and systematic is the regulation of their day, that whenever you make a demand upon them, they seem to find additional corners to offer for unselfish service. I confess as a minister that the men to whom I most hopefully look for additional service are the busiest men."

Let us face this fact squarely and without equivocation. *Each of us has the same amount of time as anyone else in the world.* Others may have more ability, more money, greater influence, but each of us has twenty-four hours each day to use. As in our Lord's parable of the talents (Matthew 25:14–30), each is entrusted with the same amount of time, but not all of us use it so as to gain a tenfold return.

True, we do not all have the same capacity, and we are not responsible for that, but that factor is taken into account in the parable. The reward for the servant with less capacity, but who was equally faithful, is the same. We are not responsible for our capacity, but we are responsible for the way in which we use our time.

When we have comparatively little to carry in a suitcase, it seems almost as full as when we have much; the less we have, the more carelessly we pack it. The person who claims to have no time is likely to be guilty of "careless packing." We should regard it as axiomatic that we have time to do the whole will of God for our lives.

Dixon E. Hoste, General Director of the China Inland Mission, lived an extremely full life, but he always made time for a deep and extensive prayer life. He made that his first priority because he deemed it most important. But he did not arrive immediately at a mastery of his time.

"It is easy to waste time," he wrote. "The missionary after breakfast may sit down to read the newspaper, or let time slip by some other way. But this cannot be done in business life. I have found the need of much watchfulness and self-discipline in this matter during my year in the interior. A sensitive conscience about the use of time needs to be maintained."

Three Constructive Suggestions

These suggestions, if followed, could be of help to those who are seriously seeking to be their best for God, and should enable them to do this without strain and tension.

Stop the leaks

It will be profitable to think of our day, not only in hours, but in smaller segments of time. If we look after the minutes, the hours will look after themselves.

Few men have packed more into a lifetime than Frederick B. Meyer. Like John Wesley, he divided his days into spaces of five minutes, and chided himself if one passed in idleness. For us ordinary mortals this would impose intolerable strain, but not so with Meyer. "His calm manner was not the sleep of an inactive mind," wrote his biographer, "it was more like the sleep of a spinning top. He was never in a hurry because he was always in haste."

Just a little before his death he said to a friend, "I think I am an example of what the Lord can do with a man who concentrates on one thing at a time."

Few of us can hope to achieve such a degree of concentration as to make every quarter-hour carry a full quota of usefulness, but that does not excuse us from trying. For example, it is amazing how much reading can be squeezed into fragments of time redeemed from the trash pile.

It is vain to wait until we get periods of time to read seriously; we must make and take the time to read by seizing the minutes we have. From the suggested analysis of our time, we should discover any unsuspected leakages of time and, with purpose of heart, plug the leak and fill that time with something of value.

Study priorities

Much time that is not actually wasted is spent on activities that are not of primary importance. A fool has been described as a person who has missed the proportion of things. Some of us have the tendency to be so engrossed in the secondary that we have little time for the primary. So much time is expended on petty details that matters of major importance are squeezed out. And *the casualty is usually in the realm of the spiritual.* Check to see whether spiritual concerns are allotted adequate time, or whether they are relegated to a secondary place by that which is good.

Jesus Himself indicated that the secret of progressive living was to sacrifice the pearl of inferior value for the pearl of transcendent worth. Are we doing the most important things, or do we procrastinate where they are concerned? Weigh carefully the respective values of the opportunities and responsibilities that claim your attention. Quit altogether, or give a very minor place to things of minor importance.

John Wesley used to say, "Never be unemployed, and never be triflingly employed." But *disciplined relaxation and recreation are not of secondary importance.* People who make provision in their schedules for the renewal of physical and nervous powers are not triflingly employed. Jesus relaxed at the well in the midst of His busy ministry. Had He not done so, He would have missed the Samaritan woman. He enjoyed ordinary social life and did not consider it a waste of time to attend weddings or feasts. They were part of His Father's plan, and could be turned to good account.

Start planning your days

Without a plan, it is easy to drift. If our life is indeed a plan of God, appropriate work awaits us each hour. John R. Mott, who packed a prodigious amount into his days, used to devote half an hour now and again to laying plans for the days ahead, and he considered it time well invested. In the attitude of prayer ask, "How can I best plan today?"

We all have certain duties and obligations that demand a place. Then, certain secondary things (which should be pruned to a minimum) must be fitted in. When two duties pull in opposite directions, choose the one that seems more important. If a secular claim crowds the spiritual, do not concede the point unless you have good reason to do so.

In most of our lives there are gaps that seem too short to fill with something important. These gaps should be filled. Why not write a note or letter? Make a telephone call to someone in need. Don't wait until you get time to write. That is the devil's recipe for an unwritten letter.

Buy up the spare minutes as the miser hoards his money. The foregoing considerations may be a stimulus to some, but to others of a different disposition they may only increase the problem. While it is good to have a sensitive conscience, it is bad to have a weak and wavering conscience. The latter requires instruction and discipline, or it may exert a harmful tyranny. We need a balanced view of time or we will work under undue strain. There are cautions to be observed. Ponder these considerations.

- After we have done all in our power to the best of our ability, a vast area of need will still remain. That can be left with God.
- We are responsible only for those things over which we have control. The rest is God's concern.
- We cannot meet every call of need. We must come to terms with the possible.
- To set impossible goals only puts us under stress and produces a load of guilt when we fail to attain them.
- Circumstances may hinder us from carrying out our plan, but that is no reason for self-accusation.
- If we are unduly harassed and pressured, the time has arrived to take stock of our commitments and refuse more than we can discharge without undue strain.
- In planning, make provision for punctuality. Set your whole schedule ten minutes earlier, and that will obviate one cause of stress.

Motivation

If we are to effect a radical change in our use of time, it will take strength of purpose and a real dependence on the Lord for His enabling. Not all of us possess inflexible wills, but we can be strengthened "with power through His Spirit in our inner being" (Ephesians 3:16). Are there motives sufficiently compelling to change the pattern of our lives, to empower us to run counter to the long-established patterns of the past in regard to laxity in the use of time?

The driving force in the life of our Lord was revealed in one of His incidental sayings: "I always do what pleases him" (John 8:29). Paul imitated His Master in this: "We make it our goal to please him" (2 Corinthians 5:9).

Henry Martyn, who gave the world the New Testament in three major languages, found it impossible to waste an hour in his translation work. And his motivation? The vision of nations waiting for the truth locked up in the Book he was translating. The need of a lost world proved an impelling motive to redeem the hours—to make the best use of his time.

> *No trifling in this life of mine;*
> *Not this the path the blessed Master trod;*
> *But every hour and power employed*
> *Always and all for God.*

CHAPTER 14

Authentic Spiritual Leadership

*"The greatest among you should be like the youngest, and
the one who rules like the one who serves. . . . I am
among you as one who serves" (LUKE 22:26, 27).*

The health and prosperity of any church or organization is directly related to the quality of its leadership. Water will rise no higher than its source. It is therefore important that those in leadership should endeavor to keep on improving their potential, whether they fill a prominent or a minor role. We are under obligation to be our best for God. Paul emphasized this to the Roman Christians: "If you are a leader, exert yourself to lead" (Romans 12:8, NEB).

In referring to the prevalence of mediocre leadership, William Barclay diagnosed the situation in these words: "There are fewer and fewer with a sense of responsibility and service, who are willing to give up their leisure and pleasure to undertake leadership. In many cases unfitness is pleaded, when the real reason is disinclination."

In Scripture God is frequently represented as searching for a man of a certain type for His service:

> "The LORD has sought out a man after his own heart"
> (1 SAMUEL 13:14).

"Go up and down the streets of Jerusalem . . . search through her squares. If you can find but one person who deals honestly and seeks the truth. . ." (JEREMIAH 5:1).

"I looked for a man among them who would build up the wall and stand before me in the gap on behalf of the land" (EZEKIEL 22:30).

When God does discover such a man or woman who conforms to His spiritual requirements, it seems as though there is nothing He will not do for and through such a one, despite his or her weakness and limitations.

At this juncture in history, the church needs, more than anything else, a leadership that is authoritative, spiritual, and sacrificial. *Authoritative*, because people love to be led by one who knows where he is going. *Spiritual*, because a leadership that is unspiritual and can be explained on the level of the natural will result in sterility and spiritual bankruptcy. *Sacrificial*, because it is modeled on the life of One who gave His life as a sacrifice for the whole world, and who taught that the path to leadership was blood-stained.

The Nature of Spiritual Leadership

Leadership is influence, the ability of one person to influence others. He can lead them only to the extent that he can influence them to follow. The true nature of spiritual leadership is indicated in a sentence from the pen of Samuel M. Zwemer: "There never was a world in greater need of men and women who know the way, can keep ahead, and draw others to follow." If we are to become good leaders, it will be because we can show the way to others, the way we have ourselves successfully trodden. Because we have qualified in this area, we can secure the cooperation of others in achieving some work for God.

In some sense, leadership principles are unchanging in any age, for there is a remarkable similarity in God's dealings with people in both the Old and New Testaments. But rapidly changing conditions are affecting the context of our leadership.

Spiritual leadership is a blending of natural and spiritual qualities. Even the natural qualities are not self-produced but God-given, and they therefore reach their highest potential when they are employed in the Lord's service and for His glory.

Spirituality alone will not make one a leader; there must be a basis of natural leadership qualities. To these the Holy Spirit adds the spiritual dimension in the form of spiritual gifts.

The spiritual leader influences others, not by the power of his personality alone, but by that personality irradiated and interpenetrated by the Holy Spirit. Because the Spirit is accorded undisputed control of the life, the Spirit's power can flow through him to others. Such leadership is a matter of superior spiritual power, and that is never self-generated.

To the question, "Are leaders born or made?" there have been a variety of answers. Perhaps the correct one is "both." Such leadership is "an elusive and electric quality" that comes directly from God. On the other hand, inherent leadership skills can be cultivated and developed.

In his book *Operation Victory,* Field Marshal Montgomery enunciates seven ingredients of military leadership that are equally applicable to spiritual leadership.

> He should be able to sit back and avoid getting immersed in detail.
> He must not be petty.

He must not be pompous.

He must be a good picker of men.

He should trust those under him and let them get on with the job without interference.

He must have the power of clear decision.

He should inspire confidence.

Few Christian leaders have had greater experience in selecting and training leaders than John R. Mott. His tests for leadership are:

Does he do little things well?

Has he learned the meaning of priorities?

How does he use his leisure?

Has he intensity?

Has he learned how to take advantage of momentum?

Has he the power of growth?

What is his attitude toward discouragement?

How does he face the impossible situation?

What are his weakest points?

These lists constitute a measuring rod for evaluating our own leadership.

There is a military organization known as "Officers' Selection and Appraisal Center" (OSAC), where men are tested for leadership. When a man arrives, be he captain or private, he becomes just a number. All ranks are leveled. Each washes dishes and shines shoes like the other.

What is observed is not knowledge or proficiency, but reactions to the unexpected, to uncongenial conditions, or criticism or crisis. Each man is constantly interviewed, scrutinized, and tested to discern his leadership caliber.

God also has His OSAC, and oftentimes, all unknown to ourselves, we disqualify ourselves for more responsible service by our reactions to the tests to which He subjects us.

Qualifications for Leadership

Of course the most important factor in leadership is the leader himself or herself. The supremely important quality is *spirituality*. "The spiritual man makes judgments about all things" (1 Corinthians 2:15), Paul said. In reference to a disciplinary matter in the Corinthian church, he counseled, "If someone is caught in a sin, you who are spiritual should restore him gently" (Galatians 6:1). Even for a social service, the apostles stipulated that the men chosen should be "filled with the Spirit and wisdom."

Spirituality is the influence of the Holy Spirit in the life of the believer. To be "filled with the Spirit" is to be "controlled" by the Spirit, for that is the basic meaning of the word. A "spiritual" person is one whose mind, heart, will, and personality are possessed and controlled by the Holy Spirit. This is a *sine qua non* for spiritual leadership.

The leader should be a person of *deep humility.* This quality is neither required nor coveted in politics or commerce. Indeed, it would be a disqualification. In the words at the head of this chapter, the Master gave His conception of the path to leadership. Gentile kings might be pompous, but the man who is great in the kingdom of God will be humble like his Master, who said: "Whoever wants to be great among you must be your servant, and whoever wants to be first must be your slave" (Matthew 20:26, 27). One of the secrets of the greatness of John the Baptist is enshrined in his declaration, "He must become greater; I must become less" (John 3:30). The humility of the leader should be an ever-increasing quality. It is instructive to note Paul's progress in this grace as the years passed.

> "I am the least of the apostles and do not even deserve to be called an apostle, because I persecuted the church of God" (1 CORINTHIANS 15:9).

> "I am less than the least of all God's people" (EPHESIANS 3:8).

> "Christ Jesus came into the world to save sinners—of whom I am the worst" (1 TIMOTHY 1:15).

It has been wisely said that *the future is with the disciplined.* Without discipline, other gifts, either of nature or of grace, will never reach their maximum potential. Only the disciplined person will rise to his highest powers. He will be able to lead well because he has mastered himself.

The words *disciple* and *discipline* have a common root. A leader is a person who has first submitted to an authority imposed from without, and who then imposes on himself a more rigorous discipline. Those who rebel against authority, and scorn self-discipline, seldom qualify for leadership of a high order. They shirk the sacrifice that is demanded and the divine disciplines involved.

The good leader will work while others waste time, and sometimes will pray while others play. But he will also allow time for recreation in his schedule. He will be prepared to do the hidden or distasteful job which others have avoided because it evokes no applause and wins no appreciation.

A leader must first prove to be a good and loyal follower of those over him or her in the Lord. Because leaders so discipline themselves, others will accept their discipline.

The leader will be a person of *vision*. The old prophets were called "seers" because they had a keener spiritual vision than their contemporaries. The spiritual leader views things in the light of eternity. "Vision is more than sight, or even insight. It is to see the invisible." The great biblical characters all had this quality in marked degree.

Because he sees further than his fellows, the leader will set the standard high, will endeavour to hold them to the highest, and will encourage them not to sacrifice the ultimate for the immediate.

The leader will be someone of *clear decision*. Once sure of the will of God, he will move into prompt action, regardless of the consequences. Because his aim is single and his motives pure, his decisions are not complex and he does not vacillate.

Each of the worthies in God's Roll of Honor (Hebrews 11) was a man or woman of vision and decision. They first saw the vision, then counted the cost involved, made their decisions and acted on them. The Roll of Honor is still open.

In one of his last messages before his death in an air accident, Fred Mitchell, the British Home Director of the China Inland Mission, said this:

> It is the quality of leaders that they can bear to be sat on, absorb shocks, act as a buffer, bear being much plagued. . . . The wear and tear and the continual friction that come to the servant of God are a great test of character.

How Is Leadership Attained?

The fact that one is elected or selected for a task does not automatically make him a leader. The highest type of leader seldom seeks place or position. The position usually comes to those who, by spirituality, character, and ability, have proved themselves worthy of it.

Not all who aspire to leadership are prepared to pay the price involved. But we must comply with God's conditions in secret before He will honor us in public.

Cautions to Heed

The possession of delegated spiritual authority will not render a man or woman infallible. Because we are all "compassed with infirmity," we will be prone to make some mistakes. But a sincere mistake is not necessarily a sin. It is better to have made an honest mistake than to have attempted nothing for God. Even apostles made mistakes that God overruled.

It should be remembered that a leader is not made immune from the operation of natural laws. If he breaks physical laws, he will pay the physical penalty. Many godly men and women have broken temporarily under almost intolerable burdens. It is not without comfort to note that the two men who conversed with the Lord on the Mount of Transfiguration both cracked under the strain of their ministry and prayed that they might die. But they didn't die, and after recuperating they continued their ministry.

Spiritual leadership, once bestowed, is not automatically retained. Paul was under no illusions on this score. In his letter to the Corinthians, he tells of his godly fear of being disapproved at the last (1 Corinthians 9:27).

It seems that God deals more stringently with leaders than with their followers. Because their responsibilities keep them in the public eye as God's representatives, God's honor is involved.

But there is a complementary truth. Although God may deal severely with the erring leader, He also deals severely with those who challenge the authority of a leader He has appointed. When the sons of Korah gathered against Moses and Aaron and said, "You have gone too far! The whole community is holy, every one of them. . . . Why then do you set yourselves above the LORD's assembly?" (Numbers 16:3), divine vindication was swift: "The earth opened its mouth and swallowed them." God is jealous for those He has endorsed.

Even when Moses' sister, Miriam, criticized him for his choice of a wife, God smote her with leprosy, which then was healed through Moses' intercession.

It remains to be said that the path of the leader is often a lonely one, for he must keep ahead of his followers. The mental anguish sometimes involved in making an unpopular decision, or a decision involving a person's future, can be fully known only by those called on to do it. But even then, to do the will of God always brings its own reward, even though through tears.

CHAPTER 15

Praying with Authority

*"I have given you authority . . . to overcome all
the power of the enemy"* (LUKE 10:19).

*"How can anyone enter a strong man's house and carry
off his possessions unless he first ties up the strong man?
Then he can rob his house"* (MATTHEW 12:29).

*I*n one sense prayer cannot be analyzed, since it is a unity
and the outpouring of the life of the one who prays. Yet
there is another sense in which it can be divided into its con-
stituent elements. While prayer is one, it is also multiform.

A well-balanced prayer life will include these five elements:

Adoration—the soul lost in wondering worship of
God, especially for what He is in Himself.

Thanksgiving—the heart overflowing in grateful
appreciation of His many gifts and mercies to us.

Confession—the expression in words of heartfelt
contrition, of a sense of sin, and failure to attain the
divine standard.

Petition—the laying of personal needs before a loving heavenly Father.

Intercession—the request of one on behalf of others
who may stand in the same position of privilege, or
who do not enjoy the same access into the presence of

God. In intercession the believer stands as an intermediary between God and man. He forgets himself and his own needs in his identification with the needs of the one for whom he prays. Praying with spiritual authority would come within this category.

Within the ministry of intercession there may be contrasting spiritual activity. Our intercession may be the calm expression of a restful faith—"Ask and it will be given to you" (Matthew 7:7). Or it may be expressed in spiritual conflict: "I want you to know how much I am struggling for you and for those at Laodicea" (Colossians 2:1). "Epaphras . . . sends greetings. He is always wrestling in prayer for you" (Colossians 4:12). "We wrestle . . . against principalities [and] powers" (Ephesians 6:12, KJV).

This latter aspect of prayer is little known and less practiced by Christians today, but the mastery of what has been termed "spiritual warfare" will turn defeat into victory in many a difficult situation.

The Spirit-controlled Christian, Paul asserts, is involved in spiritual warfare with powerful but intangible and invisible forces. In this conflict only spiritual weapons will prevail, but they are available and "have divine power to demolish strongholds" (2 Corinthians 10:4). Of these weapons, the most powerful is "pray[er] in the Spirit on all occasions" (Ephesians 6:18).

In Matthew 12:28–29 and Luke 11:21–22, our Lord was trenchantly refuting the ridiculous charge of the Pharisees that He was exorcising demons by the power of the prince of the demons. As though the devil would be so naive as to destroy his own kingdom! Jesus pointed out that surely His casting out of demons indicated His mastery of their prince, rather than subservience to him.

Delegated Authority

Jesus made a startling statement to His seventy eager disciples who had returned, elated, from their evangelistic foray. Later, He asserted that all celestial and terrestrial authority had been given to Him (Matthew 28:18). Then He said to them:

> "I saw Satan fall like lightning from heaven. *I have given you authority* to trample on snakes and scorpions *and to overcome all the power of the enemy*" (LUKE 10:18–19, emphasis added).

The unmistakable inference is that this tremendous delegation of spiritual authority was that, as they believed His Word and exercised the authority He had delegated to them, they would see the overthrow of Satan in the area of their ministry. Nor had they been disappointed, for the radiant evangelists reported, "Lord, even the demons submit to us in your name" (Luke 10:17).

This promise of spiritual authority over the powers of darkness has never been withdrawn. But a short time later, when the disciples apparently lost vital faith in Christ's assurance, they found themselves impotent when confronted with a demon-possessed boy (Matthew 17:19). They were paralyzed by their own unbelief.

The Strong Man

Jesus depicted two powerful antagonists—"a strong man," and "someone stronger than he." The strong man has a palace in which he keeps his possessions safe, but only until someone stronger than himself attacks and overcomes him.

The strong man is, of course, the devil, whose power over the minds and souls of men, although great, is limited. The One stronger than he is the Lamb, through whose blood we can overcome the devil (Revelation 12:11).

The Lamb is engaged in truceless warfare with the strong man, and He will not rest until he is finally and irrevocably overcome and his palace spoiled. In this conflict between rival kingdoms, the intercessor fills an important role. But to do his part effectively, he or she must constantly recognize and count on the victory Christ gained over Satan on the cross (Colossians 2:15).

It was the discovery of this aggressive aspect of prayer that turned defeat into victory in the experience of the apostle to the Lisu people of southwest China, James O. Fraser. He had worked for five years with great devotion and self-sacrifice, but with little to show for it. Not only was he discouraged in his work, but he had almost reached the point of desperation in his own inner experience. Deliverance and blessing came through reading an article in a magazine that had been sent to him. Here is his account:

> What it showed me was that deliverance from the power of the evil one comes through definite resistance on the ground of the cross. I had found that much of the spiritual teaching one hears does not seem to work. My apprehension at any rate of other aspects of truth had broken down. The passive side of leaving everything to the Lord Jesus as our life, while blessedly true, was not all that was needed just then. . . . We need different truth at different times. Definite resistance on the ground of the cross was what brought me light, for I found that it worked. I found that I *could* have victory in the spiritual realm whenever I wanted it. . . . One had to learn gradually how to use this new-found weapon of resistance.

Being an engineer by profession, Mr. Fraser was always interested in seeing things work, and as he began to apply this truth so new to him, he was thrilled to find he had not been misled. Not only did new victory come into his life, but the longed-for blessing was poured out upon his beloved Lisu, a trickle that grew into a mighty stream.

First Bind—Then Spoil

Failure to recognize the priority stated in Matthew 12:29 can be a potent cause of lack of success in our witness. Christ said we must first bind—tie up—the strong man, and then we will be in a position to enter his palace and deliver his captives. Are we at pains to observe this order, or do we unsuccessfully try to plunder his palace while he is still unfettered? If so, small wonder if he has snatched back souls we have endeavored to deliver from his clutches.

It is this heartbreaking experience that has discouraged so many missionaries who have seen people make professions of faith, and then have watched them sucked back into the vortex of heathenism.

What is meant by the expression "binding" or "tying up" the strong man? Consider the ways in which Jesus bound him. Jesus had three major encounters with the devil—in the desert, in Gethsemane, and on Golgotha.

In the desert, He achieved His first victory by successfully resisting the three temptations that assailed Him along the three avenues by which it can reach man—appetite, avarice, ambition. Each phase of the assault He rebutted with the sword of the Spirit skillfully wielded. The devil, vanquished, left Him victor on the field.

Because of this triumph, Jesus was able to claim, "The prince of this world is coming. He has no hold on me" (John 14:30). We shall be powerless to effect the practical binding of Satan if there are unyielded areas in our lives that give him a hold over us.

Christ's next major encounter with Satan was in the *Garden of Gethsemane*. So intense and agonizing was this conflict that, contrary to nature, the blood forced its way through His pores. How did He triumph on this occasion? By merging His will with that of His Father. Note the striking progress in His prayers:

> "Father, if you are willing, take this cup from me; yet not *my* will, but *yours* be done" (LUKE 22:42, emphasis added).

> "My Father, if it is not possible for this cup to be taken away unless I drink it, *may your will be done*" (MATTHEW 26:42, emphasis added).

> "Shall I not drink the cup the Father has given me?" (JOHN 18:11).

Thus Satan suffered another shattering blow, as the Lord refused to move from complete and joyous acceptance of the will of the Father, even though it involved the cross. If we are to experience a similar victory, this will be our attitude too.

The complete and final victory over the devil was consummated *on Golgotha,* where Christ triumphed over him in the cross:

> "Having disarmed the powers and authorities, he made a public spectacle of them, triumphing over them by the cross" (COLOSSIANS 2:15).

The very purpose of the Incarnation was that "by his death he might destroy him who holds the power of death—that is, the devil" (Hebrews 2:14).

The word *destroy* here means "to render inoperative, to put out of action." The same idea is involved in the exhortation to bind the strong man. *The cross forever broke the power of the devil over the believer.* Henceforth he was a usurper. Any power he now exercises over the Christian is either because we fail to appropriate Christ's triumph on our behalf, or is the result of tolerated sin in our lives. Let us firmly grasp the fact that Christ has bound the devil in this sense, and as members of His body we may participate in His victory. His triumph becomes ours.

Potential and Actual

How does this triumph over Satan become actual and operative in the sphere of our special concern? It is not sufficient to know that on the cross Jesus potentially delivered all power. The potential must become actual, and this is when, in faith, we exercise the spiritual authority delegated to us.

In Luke 10:18–19, Jesus linked the delegation of authority over all the power of the enemy with the overthrow of Satan. As the Seventy exercised that authority, acted on Christ's assurance, they experienced the triumph He promised, and they were able to spoil the devil's palace and deliver his captives.

But in doing this we must be sure of our ground. Acts 19:13–16 records how the sons of Sceva, who were exorcists, attempted to exorcise demons "in the name of Jesus." They were attempting to exercise an authority they did not possess. The evil spirit answered them:

"'Jesus I know, and I know about Paul, but who are you?' Then the man who had the evil spirit jumped on them and overpowered them all."

It is a solemn thing to pretend an authority that has not been conferred on us by God. The powers of darkness are not to be treated lightly.

Jesus was well-known to the demons, and feared by them too. "What do you want with us, Jesus of Nazareth?" they asked. "Have you come to destroy us? I know who you are—the Holy One of God" (Mark 1:24) was their unsolicited testimony. For thirty years they had watched His sinless life, and knew they had no hold over Him.

They were acquainted with Paul too. Had they not been dismayed at his complete transformation on the Damascus road, which turned him into their most dreaded foe? Yes, they were acquainted with Paul, but they did not know these vagabond Jews. Their names were not known in hell.

Needless Impotence

The father of the demon-possessed boy lamented the impotence of the very disciples to whom Christ had delegated authority over all the power of the enemy. "Why couldn't we drive it out?" they asked Jesus. He diagnosed the cause in one word—"unbelief." They had no vital faith that He had, in reality, given them that authority, and they were powerless because of their unbelief (Matthew 17:20–21).

When we are in a similar situation for which our human power is inadequate, it is for us, making use of Christ's authority, to claim the victory He won, and maintain that attitude until it becomes manifest. Is this not what Paul meant by fighting "the good fight of faith"?

God taught this lesson to James O. Fraser as, with deepening conviction, he claimed in prayer more than one hundred Lisu families for Christ. He wrote:

> Satan's tactics seem to be as follows: he will first of all oppose our breaking through to the place of faith, for it is an authoritative "notice to quit." He does not so much mind carnal, rambling prayers, for they do not hurt him much. That is why it is so difficult to attain to a definite faith in God for a definite object. We often have to strive and wrestle in prayer (Ephesians 6:10) before we attain this quiet restful faith. And until we break right through and *join hands with God,* we have not attained to real faith at all.... However, once we attain to a *real faith,* all the forces of hell are impotent to annul it.... The real battle begins when the prayer of faith is offered.

So, making use of the Christian's authority and participating in His victory, we can be instrumental in "binding the strong man" in any given situation. Only then will we be able to permanently deliver those he holds captive.

CHAPTER 16

Weapons of Spiritual Warfare

"Though we live in the world, we do not wage war
as the world does. The weapons we fight with are
not the weapons of the world. On the contrary,
they have divine power to demolish strongholds"
(2 CORINTHIANS 10:3–4).

Whether conscious of it or not, the Christian is engaged in spiritual warfare against "the rulers, against the authorities, against the powers of this dark world, and against the spiritual forces of evil in the heavenly realms" (Ephesians 6:12). The word *campaign* would more accurately express Paul's meaning in the verse at the head of this chapter, for there is a difference between a battle and a campaign. Battles may be lost, and yet the campaign won.

The warfare of which Paul is speaking is real, not imaginary. His encounter with Satan was very real to Jesus. It is *spiritual* and not fleshly, and is not waged on the plane or after the methods of the natural man. It is *intangible*, "not against flesh and blood." We cannot lay hands on our foe. Only spiritual methods and weapons will avail. It is *interminable*. It began in the Garden of Eden, and will end only when Satan is finally bound.

In view of the vast power he wields in the world, insufficient attention is paid to the methods and activities of the devil. We allow him to outwit us in strategy and out-maneuver us in tactics, largely because we are culpably ignorant of his devices. Too much ground is lost by default because we are not alert to his insidious wiles.

In World War II, victory was won by Field Marshal Montgomery over his German rival, Rommel, largely because of his painstaking study of his opponent—his character, temperament, habits, and previous strategy and tactics. The knowledge gained enabled him so to plot his campaign as to take advantage of the strengths of his own position and the weaknesses of his foe.

The Campaign

The first eleven chapters of the book of the Revelation unveil the unceasing struggle between the church and the world. The remaining chapters show this outward conflict is but the manifestation on earth of the eternal war between light and darkness, between God and Satan.

> "And there was war in heaven. Michael and his angels fought against the dragon, and the dragon and his angels fought back. But he was not strong enough, and they lost their place in heaven. The great dragon was hurled down—that ancient serpent called the devil, or Satan, who leads the whole world astray.... 'They overcame him by the blood of the Lamb, and by the word of their testimony; they did not love their lives so much as to shrink from death'" (REVELATION 12:7–9, 11).

A survey of the history of the church uncovers something of Satan's mode of warfare. When persecution failed to subdue the zeal of the infant church, he incited the Judaizers to debase the Gospel of grace, and caused division through their insidious teachings. In this century, when Africa seemed well on the way to complete evangelization, he interposed the Muslim belt across the continent, between the unreached pagans and the advancing church. But he has failed to stem the Gospel advance.

The Warriors

"They overcame him."

In Revelation 12:9–10, a series of revealing names is given to our enemy. In five vivid words the Holy Spirit gives searching insight into his character and strategy.

The great dragon. To the Greek mind, the dragon was a fabulous monster, a dread and sinister power, cruel, mysterious, ferocious, malicious.

That ancient serpent. He is cunning and crafty, and works under cover. He seldom comes out into the open, but, as in Eden, hides behind someone else. He even transforms himself into an angel of light.

The devil. This designation means "slanderer, traducer." In the beginning of history he slandered God to Adam and Eve. Later he slandered Job to God. Slander is one of his most potent weapons, and he rejoices when children of God engage in this repulsive activity.

Satan. The adversary of God, the church, and the believer. He is the open enemy of all that is holy. He opposes all that is in man's highest interests or for God's greater glory.

Accuser of the brethren. "Then he showed me Joshua the high priest . . . and Satan standing at his right side to accuse him" (Zechariah 3:1).

He is the "father of lies," but he tells the truth when it suits his purpose. Not only does he accuse us to God, but he accuses us to one another. It is striking that the word used of him in Job, "going to and fro" (Job 1:7, KJV), suggests "going about as a spy"—a commentary on his sinister activities.

If this crafty and malicious adversary with his highly organized hierarchy is ranged against us, what hope have we of overcoming him? And yet the passage says "they"—the weak, sinful brethren whom he accused—overcame him.

As Christ's brethren, they sustained a blood relationship with their Lord, and this makes them a subject of Satan's hostility. He can now hurt and discredit the ascended Lord and Head of the church only through the members of His body. But the same relationship makes it possible for them to share His victory.

If we are to overcome Satan, the second most powerful being in the universe, we must see to our weapons.

The Weapons

Our Commander does not ask us to enter the battle and engage in spiritual warfare unarmed; He provides us with three invincible weapons of offense.

The judicial weapon

"They overcame him *by the blood of the Lamb*"—a weapon that derives its potency from the cross. The secret of victory is not our prowess, but our union with Christ in His death and resurrection.

The phrase "the blood of the Lamb" is not to be regarded as a magic charm, something to be introduced into prayer or sermon, thus attesting our orthodoxy and ensuring supernatural results. Nor is it to be a credulously mumbled formula nor a parroting of mystical words. "The blood of the Lamb" is the expression of an intelligent, active faith in the Lamb of God who, by shedding His blood, bruised the serpent's head and finally defeated him (Genesis 3:15). This expression is one of the most pregnant phrases in the Bible. In it are concentrated all the value and virtue of Christ's mediatorial work. Blood is life in solution.

The life of the Lamb, violently ended by sinful men, was yet voluntarily laid down. He rose from the dead and ascended to the right hand of God by virtue of His own blood, and "the blood of the Lamb" now becomes the ground of our victory. It should be noted that the word *by* in the phrase connotes "because of," rather than "by means of." Because He broke the power of Satan by shedding His blood, we who are united with Him by faith can participate in His victory. Satan has no counter-weapon.

When we plead in prayer the blood of the Lamb, we are really affirming that our faith is fixed and resting for victory on all that He achieved for us by His vicarious death and victorious resurrection, which released limitless divine power. *This is our first weapon of offense.*

The evidential weapon

"They overcame him . . . *by the word of their testimony*" (emphasis added).

Faith in the redemption achieved by His death is to be followed by testimony to His living and powerful Word. It is not clear whether the reference is to the Word to which they bore testimony, or to their testimony itself. Probably it is their testimony to the One who shed His blood that is in view.

Any testimony that is not Bible-based and Christ-centered will be powerless to achieve lasting spiritual results. Grounded in the Word, it becomes "the sword of the Spirit." Note that it is not argument or denunciation that silences the devil; it is testimony. The word of Christ and His apostles, tested in experience, becomes testimony.

The Word *in the intellect* is not sufficient in this warfare with Satan. Testimony occupied an all-important place in apostolic preaching, and Paul used it with great effect. There is room for medicine, agriculture, and education in the missionary program, but nothing can take the place of the word of our testimony spoken in the power of the Spirit.

God has made the world wonderfully accessible to us, and has given wings to our testimony. Radio, television, and recordings are all being used by Him to overcome the dragon.

The sacrificial weapon

"They did not love their lives so much *as to shrink from death*" (emphasis added)

The Greek word translated "testimony" is that from which we get our own word *martyr*. How often in the early church—and indeed in our own times—the testimony has led to martyrdom.

This third weapon, as distinct from the other two, is not directed at our enemy, but at our own breast. The word of testimony from one who has the martyr spirit is mightily effective. To him or her, life is of secondary importance.

In this respect Jesus set a shining example to His followers. The sacrifice of His life did not begin at Calvary, or even at Bethlehem. He was "the Lamb that was slain from the creation of the world" (Revelation 13:8). He was the perfect exemplification of His own teaching that "unless a kernel of wheat falls to the ground and dies, it remains only a single seed. But if it dies, it produces many seeds" (John 12:24). The word of our testimony will be sterile unless we, like the Master, are treading the way of the Cross.

It is not too much to say that in our affluent western lands there is no single thing so absent from contemporary Christianity as this sacrificial, this martyr spirit. Being a Christian today in the main confers benefits rather than cost and sacrifice. We are closely wedded to our comforts. Is it appropriate that the cross-bearing Lord should be followed by cross-shirking disciples?

The Victory

"They overcame him."

We close this chapter on a note of undefeatable optimism. Jesus stated categorically:

> "On this rock I will build my church, and the gates of Hades will not overcome it" (MATTHEW 16:18).

Satan's judgment and defeat were finally secured at the cross, but until the sentence on him is finally executed, we have in our hands these invincible weapons. We count on the victory of Calvary and the One who accomplished it. We hear testimony to its conquering power. Are we willing to lay down life itself for our Redeemer?

CHAPTER 17

The Secret of Spiritual Fervor

"If anyone else thinks he has reasons to put confidence in the flesh, I have more . . . as for zeal, persecuting the church" (PHILIPPIANS 3:4, 6).

"His disciples remembered that it is written: 'Zeal for your house will consume me'" (JOHN 2:17).

Zeal is not a distinctively Christian word, yet it has an honorable place in the Christian vocabulary. It can be exhibited in any of life's activities, whether secular or sacred. People who have achieved great things in the service of God or man possessed a consuming fervor and zeal that enabled them to overleap all obstacles in the pursuit of their goal.

Zeal of the right sort is a quality to be coveted. The meaning of the word is "ardor, enthusiasm in the pursuit of anything, ardent and active interest, fervor." Unfortunately, the word that connotes such desirable qualities has become somewhat debased in meaning. It is often attributed to someone who is very enthusiastic, but rather lacking in balance and intelligence.

Jesus displayed this quality to a unique degree from His early years. It was zeal for His Father's house and interests that drew the undeserved rebuke from His parents when He was only twelve years old (Luke 2:49). Throughout His whole life this fervor persisted unabated, until it led Him to the cross.

Misdirected Zeal

Much that passes as spiritual zeal is only fleshly energy—soulish rather than spiritual. Religious zeal is by no means confined to evangelical believers. Did ever a religious group display more feverish zeal than do Jehovah's Witnesses?

Paul was not lacking in zeal before his conversion, but it was tragically misdirected. "I was . . . just as zealous for God as any of you are today" (Acts 22:3), he protested. But his zeal led him into tragic excesses.

> "On the authority of the chief priests I put many of the saints in prison, and when they were put to death, I cast my vote against them. Many a time I went from one synagogue to another to have them punished. . . . In my obsession against them I even went to foreign cities to persecute them" (ACTS 26:10–11).

After his experience on the Damascus road, his mistaken zeal was one of his greatest sorrows. "I am the least of the apostles and do not even deserve to be called an apostle, because I persecuted the church of God" (1 Corinthians 15:9). He could never forgive himself, but he reveled in the forgiving grace of God. Misdirected zeal can and does work havoc with the church of God.

Misunderstood Zeal

Because He was so conspicuously different from all other men, Christ's foes described Him as a demoniac. "Why are you trying kill me?" He asked the Jews. "'You are demon-possessed,' the crowd answered. 'Who is trying to kill you?'" (John 7:20).

His zeal perplexed even His friends, but they put a more charitable construction on His unusual words and actions. "When his family heard about this, they went to take charge of him, for they said, 'He is out of his mind.'" How astounding that the only perfectly balanced man should be so regarded, even by His family.

The word *zeal* is derived from the Greek word "to boil," and signifies an ardor, an enthusiasm that spontaneously and irresistibly boils up in the heart.

When the disciples saw their Master ablaze with holy zeal and flaming with sinless anger, disturbing the rhythm of the centuries by driving the rapacious money-changers and traders from the temple (Psalm 69:9), they suddenly realized the meaning of the prophecy: "Zeal for your house will consume me" (John 2:17).

In the detailed instructions Jesus gave to the Twelve when He sent them out on a Gospel foray, Jesus warned them of what lay ahead.

> "A student is not above his teacher, nor a servant above his master. It is enough for the student to be like his teacher, and the servant like his master. If the head of the house has been called Beelzebub, how much more the members of his household!" (MATTHEW 10:24–25).

It was not strange, then, that Paul should share the misunderstanding of his master. "At this point Festus interrupted Paul's defense. 'You are out of your mind, Paul!' he shouted. 'Your great learning is driving you insane'" (Acts 26:24).

Is it not amazing that the apostle of Christian sanity should be considered unbalanced because of his spiritual fervor? It is true that, compared with others of his day, Paul's actions were hardly normal, but sanity is a relative term. It all depends on who does the judging!

It was not standard practice to act as Paul did in Ephesus. "Be on your guard," he told the Ephesians. "Remember that for three years I never stopped warning each of you night and day with tears" (Acts 20:31). But was this not evidence of the truest sanity? Paul had both this world and the next in true perspective, and acted accordingly.

> Lord, give me this very day a burning zeal. For souls immortal, enable me to plead with such, with earnestness intense, love strong as death, and faith God-given. Will the world cry, "Mad"? I would be mad; such madness be my joy. For thrice it blesses; first my own cold heart, then glorifies my God, and plucks perchance my sin-stained brother from the jaws of death.
>
> ANONYMOUS

In Romans 12 the apostle exhorts the believers not to slacken in their zeal, and in the same chapter he encourages them to cultivate Christian sanity (v. 3). So in his thinking, zeal and sanity were not necessarily mutually exclusive.

"For as God in his grace has enabled me, I charge every one of you not to think more highly of himself than he ought to think, but to cultivate Christian sanity, according as God has given to every man faith as a measure" (Romans 12:3, E. M. Blaiklock translation). Here Paul is deprecating undue self-esteem and inculcating sane thinking. The word he uses, *sophrosune,* combines the ideas of moderation and self-control, that delicate balance of mind that does not fly to extremes. And yet this is the man who is accused of being mad because of his excess of zeal for his Master.

Genuine Zeal

In writing of true zeal and false, A. W. Tozer contrasted the pure love of God that expresses itself in a burning desire to advance God's glory, and the eternal welfare of men, with the "nervous and squirrel-cage" activity of selfish and ambitious church leaders.

The genuine zeal has Christ as its object. Of this the motto of Count Nikolaus Zinzendorf is a good example. "I have one passion; it is He, He alone." His Christ-centered zeal sparked the great Moravian missionary church and a prayer chain that operated day and night for a hundred years.

In his great poem, *St. Paul,* F. W. H. Myers explains Paul's glowing zeal in these words:

> *Christ, I am Christ's, and let that name suffice you,*
> *Ay, for me too He greatly has sufficed;*
> *Lo, with no winning words would I entice you,*
> *Paul has no honor and no friend but Christ.*
> *Yea, through life, death, thro' sorrow and thro' sinning,*
> *He shall suffice me, for He hath sufficed;*
> *Christ is the end, for Christ is the beginning,*
> *Christ the beginning, for the end is Christ.*

Christ-centered zeal will manifest itself in various ways. It moved Paul to seek souls night and day with tears. It drove Epaphras to intense prayer for his fellow-Christians at Colosse. Paul wrote of him: "He is always wrestling in prayer for you, that you may stand firm in all the will of God" (Colossians 4:12).

It produced in the poor Macedonian colonists a provocative liberality. "They gave as much as they were able, and even beyond their ability. . . . They urgently pleaded with us for the privilege of sharing in this service" (2 Corinthians 8:3, 4).

Paul's ideal for his converts as reflected in his prayers was that they might have

A mind aflame with the truth of God.
A heart aglow with love for God and man.
A will ablaze with passion for the glory of God.

It is true that we evangelicals can do with more genuine scholarship, but much more do we need an incandescent zeal for God. The combination of deep scholarship and flaming zeal may be rare, but they are not incompatible, and together they are irresistible.

The brilliant Cambridge scholar, Henry Martyn, who at the age of twenty was awarded the highest honor the world had to give in the area of mathematics, said that to his amazement, he felt he had grasped only a shadow. But when for the first time he stood on Indian soil, he said, "Now let me burn out for God." Within seven years his zeal had consumed him, but not before he had translated the New Testament into three major languages. And that was no shadow! His prayer inspired these words:

And when I am dying, how glad I shall be
That the lamp of my life has been blazed out for Thee.
I shall not care in whatever I gave
Of labor or money one sinner to save.
I shall not care that the way has been rough,
That Thy dear feet led the way is enough.
And when I am dying, how glad I shall be,
That the lamp of my life has been blazed out for Thee.

Maintained Zeal

Archbishop H. C. Lees gave a felicitous translation of Romans 12:11. For the central clause, "fervent in spirit" in the

King James Version, he gave, "Kept at boiling point by the Holy Spirit." The inference is that between our diligence in the service of man (v. 11a) and our bondservice for the Master (v. 11c), there is a central furnace to keep our spirits "fairly seething with enthusiasm." It is comparatively easy at times of special blessing to come to boiling point, but it is quite another matter to stay there.

We can neither generate nor maintain our own zeal. If it is not to "flag," there must be some external stimulus, and this is provided by the Holy Spirit. The power generated must not be allowed to evaporate in unutilized steam, but be harnessed to do bondservice for the Master.

It is of supreme importance, then, that we maintain a correct relationship with the Holy Spirit, and that we do not grieve Him.

When Christian, in Bunyan's *Pilgrim's Progress,* approached the Interpreter's house, he saw a fire on the hearth; but to his surprise, although a man was pouring on water, the flames only leaped higher. The phenomenon mystified him until he went behind, and saw there another man pouring on oil. Mystery solved!

It is the work of the gracious Holy Spirit constantly to pour oil on the fire and keep our zeal at boiling point. Apollos was a glowing example of His ministry. "He spoke with great fervor and taught about Jesus accurately" (Acts 18:25).

Fifty days after the resurrection the facts of the Gospel were all complete and were common knowledge. But nothing significant happened until the descent of the *Holy Spirit.* When He came, the Christians were so filled with holy passion and zeal that the Jews could explain it only as intoxication, confusing the devil's stimulant with the divine Stimulus.

How to be kept at boiling point? "Thinking enough, meditating enough, musing enough on Christ will do it," wrote Alexander Whyte. "Yes, if you will, you can think and read and pray yourself into the possession of a heart as hot as Paul's heart. For the same Holy Spirit as gave Christ His hot heart is given to you also."

CHAPTER 18

Money—Its Use and Abuse

"In everything I did, I showed you by this kind
of hard work we must help the weak, remembering the
words the Lord Jesus himself said, 'It is more blessed
to give than to receive'" (ACTS 20:35).

"Will a man rob God?" (MALACHI 3:8).

*I*n this passage, which contains the only direct statement of
our Lord outside the Gospels, He pronounced a ninth
beatitude. Taking that word in its full meaning, the thought is
that the liberal and generous giver is to be envied or congratu-
lated. He or she will always be enriched, never impoverished.
But as with the other eight beatitudes, the blessing promised is
spiritual and not always material. Not without reason did the
Holy Spirit preserve this sentence which underscores the superior blessedness.

There is often a definite connection between weakness in
the spiritual life and failure in the stewardship of money. Mul-
titudes can testify that obedience to Malachi's exhortation,
"Bring the whole tithe into the storehouse" (Malachi 3:10), has
been the prelude to the opening of the floodgates of heaven in
their spiritual experience.

Paul refers to giving to God as a "grace" that was neglected
by the Corinthian Christians.

"Just as you excel in everything—in faith, in speech, in knowledge, in complete earnestness and in your love for us—*see that you also excel in this grace of giving* "
(2 CORINTHIANS 8:7, emphasis added).

Can we say that we have both excelled in this grace and experienced this beatitude?

It is not without significance that in the three Synoptic Gospels one verse out of six, and sixteen of our Lord's thirty-five parables, are devoted directly or indirectly to money, its use or abuse. So with our Lord's example before us, we need have no inhibitions in speaking about money in relation to God's work.

Samuel Chadwick pointed out that a Jew's religion was an expensive one. We talk in these days about giving a tithe, a tenth of our income to God, and consider that at any rate we have met the demands of the ancient law. But that is not so. The tithe was only the starting point. The Jew's tithe was reckoned *after* he had given his firstfruits, which consisted of one sixth of his increase. Then every third year, a second tithe was given to the poor, besides all the special offerings of cleansing and con-secration, so that his total contribution to religion would be nearer one-fifth than one-tenth of his income (*The Christian,* 2/3/67).

An Acid Test

Money is one of the acid tests of character. For a revealing insight into someone's true character—whether rich or poor—observe his or her reaction to possessions. Like many since, the young man in Matthew 19:21–22 became the abject slave of his possessions, and thus forfeited eternal life. Instead of his having them, they possessed him so strongly that he was prepared, albeit sorrowfully, to lose his soul rather than sacrifice the temporal advantages they conferred. We all know such people today.

It is a fine art to use our money without parsimony, and yet avoid extravagance. It requires that fine spiritual balance, that "sober judgment" that Paul enjoined on the Roman Christians (Romans 12:3).

Much popular thinking about money and possessions is definitely sub-scriptural. The phrase in the parable of Matthew 25:18—"his master's money"—is significant. The basic question we should ask ourselves when considering our giving to God is not "How much of *our money* should we give to God?" but "How much of *God's money* should we keep for ourselves?" If we answer that question correctly, we shall without fail experience the ninth beatitude. Both money and the power to earn it are gifts of God. We are not owners, only stewards and trustees of our possessions.

One of the most scathing indictments in Scripture is that directed toward the Jews of Malachi's day, who "picked the pockets" of God Himself by keeping their choicest possessions for themselves, while offering to Him the worthless refuse.

> "'Will a man rob God? [He asks] Yet you rob me.'
> "But you ask, 'How do we rob you?'
> "'In tithes and offerings. You are under a curse—the whole nation of you—because you are robbing me'"
> (MALACHI 3:8, 9).

But such is the grace of God that He immediately follows His indictment with a conditional promise of overflowing blessing:

> "'Bring the whole tithe into the storehouse, that there may be food in my house. Test me in this,' says the LORD Almighty, 'and see if I will not throw open the floodgates

of heaven and pour out so much blessing that you will not have room enough for it'" (MALACHI 3:10).

Unfortunately, this type of hypocrisy is not confined to Malachi's day. Calvin lamented that the heathen contributed more to their gods to express their superstition than Christians were giving to the cause of Christ to express their love. But so, thank God, is the promised benediction being experienced when the condition is fulfilled.

The Law of the Tithe

Opposition to the practice of tithing comes, in the main, from those who are unwilling to do it! Seldom will you hear a willing tither complain!

It is not generally understood that tithing was practiced long before the law promulgated by Moses. Abraham gave to Melchizedek, priest of God Most High, "a tenth of everything" that he had captured (Genesis 14:20). The consecration of tithes was as customary with the Romans, Greeks, and Arabians as with the Jews.

The practice received divine sanction at Sinai, but we must remember that the law of the tithe antedated Moses by four hundred years. To the Jew it was an inescapable obligation.

Some believers contend that the Christian is "not under law, but under grace" (Romans 6:14), and therefore the law of the tithe has been abrogated for them. But surely we who have been redeemed "not with perishable things such as silver or gold, ... but with the precious blood of Christ" (1 Peter 1:18) do not desire to be antinomian with regard to Christian liberality! Are we not "under law" to Christ with His higher law of love? Shall we take advantage of God's love and grace to reduce our giving below the minimum level of a Jew under the law? John Chrysostom exclaimed: "Oh what a shame, that what was no great matter among the Jews should be pretended to be among Christians."

In this, as in all else, the Lord set a shining example. As a devout Jew who was punctilious in observing the law, did He not give more than one tenth of His carpenter's earnings into His Father's treasury?

Admittedly tithing is nowhere specifically commanded in the New Testament, since that is not the genius of God's method under grace. "I am not commanding you" (2 Corinthians 8:8), were Paul's words in this very context. He knew that a lavish hand without a loving heart was spiritually valueless.

In the warm glow of their experience on the Day of Pentecost, the early disciples sold their possessions and gave to anyone in need. To them, sacrificial giving to God, and for His work, was a spiritual luxury, not an irksome duty to be evaded if at all possible. The penurious widow, out of her abject poverty, gave everything, "all she had to live on" (Mark 12:44).

Provocative Liberality

The model of Christian stewardship of money Paul held up before the richly gifted but ungenerous Corinthian church was the poverty-stricken church in Macedonia. They were remarkable people!

> "Out of the most severe trial, their overflowing joy and their extreme poverty welled up in rich generosity. For I testify that they gave as much as they were able, and even beyond their ability. Entirely on their own, *they urgently pleaded with us* for the privilege of sharing in this service to the saints" (2 CORINTHIANS 8:2–4, emphasis added).

Despite their limited resources—they were colonial pioneers—they gave to the point of real sacrifice. They did not wait to be urged, but pleaded for the privilege of giving. And the spirit of liberality they displayed proved provocative (Mark 12:43); it inspired Paul to put before the church, in all ages, the supreme example of giving—that of the Lord, who gladly impoverished Himself for our enrichment (2 Corinthians 8:9).

The intrinsic value of any act is, of course, determined by its inspiring motive. If we give mainly to receive God's blessing on our business or our professional advancement, or even to receive spiritual blessing, we thereby, in large measure, neutralize our gift. As Robert G. Le Tourneau, himself a generous steward, put it "If you give because it pays to give, it will not pay." Jesus assessed the gift of the widow not so much by its quantity, as by the devotion that accompanied it. If we give only what we can spare without affecting our comfort, that is hardly sacrificial giving.

The Enemy, ever vigilant, endeavors to block the springs of generosity. He will dry up the fountain of liberality by suggesting *postponement of the gift* until some time when it will be easier or more convenient. But the stifling of a generous impulse today makes it easier to do the same tomorrow.

Another of his ploys is to *freeze the assets of* the truly generous-hearted person, so that he or she has little liquid cash to give. Expanding business requires an injection of capital that demands every dollar. Or more money must be put in to save existing investments. How familiar the pattern has become, and the generous person has not perceived the strategy of Satan.

When income increases, the Tempter encourages a proportional increase in the standard of living, while the amount for giving remains static.

When he earned thirty pounds a year, John Wesley lived on twenty-six and gave four. When his stipend doubled, he lived on twenty-six and gave thirty-four. Small wonder that God could trust him with spiritual riches.

Extra-Corpus Benevolence

Another stratagem of the Enemy is to short-circuit liberality by what Adoniram J. Gordon of Boston termed *extra-corpus liberality*—postponement of generosity until after death.

"Why is it," he asks, "that so many Christians make death their executor, leaving thousands and millions to be dispensed by his bony fingers? If they die, their wealth can stay behind; their covetousness can survive and reap post-mortem usury.

"It is doubtless wise to make such modest provision for our dependents as we are able, but surely it cannot be termed Christian generosity when a man waits until death shakes religious and charitable legacies from his pockets. Let us give all we can during our lifetime, and have the joy of seeing our money working for God. God promises a reward to deeds done in the body, not out of it. To be generous with God from right motives brings its recompense both here and hereafter."

The harvest we reap in the coming day will be in exact proportion to our sowing, for "whoever sows sparingly will also reap sparingly" (2 Corinthians 9:6).

There is an unfailing law of recompense that operates in favor of the generous person:

"Give, and it will be given to you. A good measure, pressed down, shaken together and running over, will be poured into your lap" (LUKE 6:38).

The converse is also true: "One man gives freely, yet gains even more; another withholds unduly, but comes to poverty. A generous man will prosper" (Proverbs 11:24, 25).

Arthur T. Pierson highlights the importance of unselfishness in giving.

> We ascend still higher to the law of unselfishness. "Do good to them, and lend to them without expecting to get anything back. Then your reward will be great" (Luke 6:35).
>
> Much of our giving is not giving at all, but only lending or exchanging. He who gives to another of whom he expects to receive as much again is not giving but trading. True giving has another's good solely in view, and hence bestows upon those who cannot and will not repay, who are too destitute to pay back. That is like God's giving to the evil and unthankful. That is giving prompted by love.
>
> *(Prairie Overcomer,* July, 1960)

One has only to listen to some television programs to realize that Dr. Pierson is not overstating the case.

It could be a wholesome exercise to examine our past stewardship, and to make any amendment the Spirit of God might suggest.

CHAPTER 19

An Optimistic View of Old Age

"Here I am today, eighty-five years old!"
(JOSHUA 14:10, NIV)

" . . . give me this mountain" (JOSHUA 14:12, KJV).

Why is it that biography occupies so large a place in the divine revelation? Is it not so that we can learn valuable spiritual lessons from the failures and successes of these real men and women who were just like us? Human biographers tend to record the best and omit the worst, but Bible biographers include the scars and wrinkles. We learn most readily when we see the truth embodied and lived out in men and women just like ourselves.

One of the model characters of the Old Testament was Caleb, the son of Jephunneh. The passing years, instead of witnessing gradual eclipse, only served to increase his stature. He demonstrated the exhilarating truth that it is possible for the greatest achievement in life to take place in old age, and that there is no arbitrarily fixed retiring age in God's service.

At every stage of life Caleb merits our emulation. In no respect does he disappoint us. His name is appropriately derived from a Hebrew word associated with fidelity, obedience, and alertness to discern his master's will—qualities in which he excelled.

As with Moses, Caleb's life divides into three clearly-defined periods. Until the age of forty, he was a slave in Egypt. Then as leader in his tribe, he was selected to explore Canaan, and then spent forty years in the desert. It was in the third period of his life that his greatest achievement took place.

He Was Zealous in Youth

Caleb appears on the stage of Israel's history as a comparatively young man, and of his early life nothing is recorded. However, from his subsequent history we are afforded insight into his character and conduct as a young man.

The only clue is found in Numbers 13:1, when each of the men called to explore the land of Canaan is said to be a leader in his tribe. That tells its own story. Leaders do not just happen. Behind the scenes there has been strong discipline and sterling character. We are told only one event in our Lord's thirty years of obscurity, but the subsequent years of holy living and selfless service tell us all we need to know about His youth. So with Caleb.

The crisis does not create, but always reveals, the man. In the crisis of shipwreck Paul was only "one of certain prisoners." But in the crisis he became undisputed master of the situation (Acts 27:13–25). The choice of Caleb as one of the spies indicates the esteem in which he was held. Of his many admirable qualities, two are conspicuous.

He displayed great courage. His moral courage was highlighted when he and Joshua stood alone against the swiftly flowing tide of popular opinion. It takes a strong person to stand alone. For young people who crave the approval of their peers, this is a stringent test. Peer pressure can be an awesome thing. Not everyone is willing to sponsor a minority cause. It is all too easy to maintain a guilty silence in an adverse theological climate.

It took no small degree of *physical courage* for Caleb to maintain his attitude of faith when "the whole assembly talked about stoning him" (Numbers 14:10). But he refused to be intimidated.

He evidenced a robust and unwavering faith in unpropitious circumstances. This quality stands high in God's scale of values (Hebrews 11:6), and Caleb's faith was the more remarkable because it flourished amid the miasmas of unbelief resulting from the pessimistic majority report of the spies:

> "The people who live there are powerful, and the cities are fortified and very large. We even saw descendants of Anak [giants]. . . . We can't attack those people; they are stronger than we are. . . . The land we explored devours those living in it. . . . We seemed like grasshoppers in our own eyes" (NUMBERS 13:28–33).

Into this chilling atmosphere of despair and unbelief, Caleb injected a shot of faith:

> "We should go up and take possession of the land, for we can certainly do it. . . . If the LORD is pleased with us, he will lead us into that land . . . Do not be afraid of the people of the land because we will swallow them up. Their protection is gone, but the LORD is with us. Do not be afraid of them" (NUMBERS 13:30; 14:8, 9).

But alas, this magnificent blending of faith and courage failed to elicit a positive response. Caleb and Joshua had seen everything the ten had seen. They had neither underestimated the power of their foes nor minimized the magnitude of the task before them. The difference lay in the fact that the ten matched the strength of the giants with their grasshopper strength, while the two matched it against the omnipotence of God. The ten gazed at the giants. Caleb and Joshua gazed at God, and difficulties dwindled before their virile faith.

Unbelief has a notoriously short memory. The ten urged the people, "We should choose a leader and go back to Egypt" (Numbers 14:4). How soon they had forgotten the taskmaster's lash! But for Caleb there was no turning back, only moving forward. His spirit was like that of David Livingstone, who said, "I am prepared to go anywhere, provided it is forward."

As we face our own personal giants and fortified cities, are we emulating the ten or the two?

He Was Consistent in Mid-Life

Midlife has its own peculiar testings in both the physical and spiritual realms. They may not be as volcanic as those of youth, but what they lose in intensity they gain in subtlety. Many who soared like a rocket in youth have descended like burnt-out sticks in middle age.

There are obvious advantages when we attain this stage of life, but there are counter-balancing dangers. It is often here that one develops a loss of fervor and a waning of personal devotion to Christ. A lukewarm sense of duty replaces ardent love. Instead of transmuting the vanishing enthusiasms of youth into a worthy life-purpose, life becomes insipid and anemic. One may weakly succumb to the temptation to ease up on self-denial and yield to softening ease. Too often, unrealized ideals in marriage and home life come to be accepted as inevitable. With the fixing of life tendencies and habits, disillusionment and cynicism become the pattern in greater or lesser degree. Unconsciously, a subtle deterioration sets in. It is easy to stop growing and striving for greater maturity.

Caleb passed the tests of youth with flying colors. How does he fare in the long drawn-out tests of middle life? "The hardest part of the journey is the middle mile." The enthusiasm of a new undertaking buoys one up at the start. There is the thrill of reaching the goal at the finish. But it is the middle mile which tests the stamina and mettle of the runner. It is then that the grace of patient continuance is most needed.

Caleb's was a singularly hard and embittering lot in the middle mile. The sin and unbelief of his contemporaries doomed him to a life of frustration and disappointment for the forty years that should have been the best of his life. The apparent reward for his faithfulness was aimless trekking in a barren desert when his powers were at their zenith.

By worldly standards he would have been justified in being petulant and resentful, but he endured the long-sustained test without losing spiritual stature. He was one of the rare souls who was never offended at God's dealings with him.

Caleb soared as an eagle in his youth. Now he has mastered the art of running without wearying. But can he walk without fainting in his old age?

He Was Adventurous in Old Age

No other Bible character presents us with such an optimistic and inspiring view of old age as does Caleb. The supreme challenge of his life came when he was eighty-five years old, the age when most are dreaming only of security and comfortable retirement. Yet the hero of forty was no less heroic at eighty-five. He demonstrated that the "tragedy" of old age can be turned into glorious achievement. To him, old age was not petering out, but pressing on to grander attainments. Not slowly descending the mountain, but scaling another peak; not senility, but adventure and achievement. His life moved on, not to termination merely, but to consummation. His last years were his best.

At every stage of life Caleb towered above his contemporaries. In his youth he stood alone. In midlife he walked alone. In old age he climbed alone.

> *For age is opportunity no less*
> *Than youth itself, though in another dress.*
> *And as the evening twilight fades away,*
> *The sky is filled with stars invisible by day.*
>
> H. W. LONGFELLOW

For forty-five years Caleb had patiently waited for the fulfillment of God's promise to him through Moses (Joshua 14:9–10). In his interview with Joshua at the partitioning of Canaan, Caleb five times made reference to the promise that had sustained him through the desert years. The passage of time had done nothing to quench his faith in God or to dampen his ardent spirit.

He was physically virile. "I am still as strong today as the day Moses sent me out" (Joshua 14:11). Few octogenarians are so fortunate! But it must be remembered that *his* was a victory of the *spirit*, not of the *body*. Not all are blessed with such physical health, but all can triumph in spirit. This old man, who should have been pulling on his slippers, was talking of binding on shoes of iron to tackle the mountain where the giants lived!

He was spiritually audacious. "Give me this mountain, whereof the LORD spake in that day" (Joshua 14:12 KJV) was his request of Joshua. Not fertile river flat, but the mountain that held fearsome giants. *He asked for the most difficult assignment in the nation!* What a man! (How different from the attitude of a young missionary who asked for an assignment where the communists would not come!) The flame of Caleb's courage had not died down even in old age. His was not careless recklessness but confident faith.

What mountain had Caleb asked for? Hebron, the most powerful stronghold of the enemy. It was a strategic city and probably the choicest spot in the land; fertile, elevated, and with a wonderful view. To him it was sacred soil, for here the patriarchs spent most of their lives. There Abraham and Sarah, Isaac and Rebekah, Jacob and Leah lay buried. Caleb would be satisfied with nothing less than the best, even though it involved dangerous conflict. Satan disputes our way most fiercely, not on the plains of the mediocre, but on the heights.

Caleb's ambitious request, "Give me this mountain," is a grand watchword for the aging Christian. As we tend to lose the spirit of adventure and aggression, and become hesitant to risk another step of faith for God, perhaps we, too, should remove our slippers and attack some menacing mountain in which the enemies of God are entrenched. We could well pray:

> "Make us thy mountaineers, we would not linger on the lower slope."

One of the most striking aspects of Caleb's triumph was that, while none of the younger men of Israel (all his contemporaries had died in the desert) succeeded in totally expelling the enemy from their territory, it is recorded that Caleb drove out the three giants of Anak (Joshua 15:14).

Two reasons were given for the failure of the younger men. *Sheer inability.* They could not drive them out (Numbers 13:31, 32). Their lack of faith resulted in lack of power. *Indolence.* "How long will you wait before you begin to take possession of the land?" (Joshua 18:3) was Joshua's complaint.

Why did Caleb prevail where these men failed? The secret is enshrined in seven words. *"I . . . followed the LORD my God wholeheartedly"* (Joshua 14:8, emphasis added), he was able to claim with a clear conscience. Moses added a similar testimony (Joshua 14:9). But the highest tribute was paid by God Himself: "My servant Caleb has a different spirit and follows me wholeheartedly" (Numbers 14:24). What higher eulogy could he have received? With him there were no divided loyalties.

There are lessons of permanent value to be learned from the life of Caleb.

- Following the Lord wholeheartedly involves a call to service.
- Claiming our inheritance in Christ will involve us in new conflict.
- Consistent obedience increases moral strength for further conflict.
- Fidelity to God's commands enriches the whole life.
- Faith is contagious, and so is unbelief.
- God is pleased with a worthy ambition.

Do we find our title much larger than the spiritual territory we actually occupy and enjoy? Are there still enemies to be subdued, giants that refuse to budge? If so, there is a reason.

Perhaps we have failed to appropriate our inheritance (Ephesians 1:3). God cannot be both giver and receiver. We obtain only those spiritual blessings we claim in faith.

Or there may be some inner reservation, something that short-circuits power and saps vitality. Complete victory comes from restful confidence and unreserved obedience.

Die climbing!

About the Author

Dr. J. Oswald Sanders served as General Director of the Overseas Missionary Fellowship (formerly China Inland Mission); he was also a Christian teacher and administrator as well as an internationally known author and speaker. During his sixty-plus years in Christian leadership, Dr. Sanders wrote more than forty books on the Christian life. He died in 1992 at the age of ninety in his native land of New Zealand.

Note to the Reader

The publisher invites you to share your response to the message of this book by writing Discovery House Publishers, Box 3566, Grand Rapids, MI 49501, USA. For information about other Discovery House books, music, or videos, contact us at the same address or call 1-800-653-8333. Find us on the Internet at http://www.dhp.org; or send e-mail to books@dhp.org.